RELIGION IN THE U.S.S.R.

THE CONTEMPORARY SOVIET UNION SERIES:
INSTITUTIONS AND POLICIES

Each volume in the Contemporary Soviet Union Series examines in detail the facts about an important aspect of Soviet rule as it has affected the Soviet citizen in the 50 years since the Bolshevik Revolution of 1917.

Subjects include industry, culture, religion, agriculture, and so on. A careful examination of official Soviet material in each field provides essential basic reading for all students of Soviet affairs.

Robert Conquest is a former Research Fellow in Soviet affairs at the London School of Economics and Political Science and Senior Fellow of Columbia University's Russian Institute. His works include *Power and Policy in the U.S.S.R.*, *The Pasternak Affair: Courage of Genius*, *Common Sense about Russia*, *The Soviet Deportation of Nationalities*, and *Russia after Khrushchev*.

THE CONTEMPORARY SOVIET UNION SERIES:

INSTITUTIONS AND POLICIES

EDITED BY ROBERT CONQUEST

Religion
in the U.S.S.R.

FREDERICK A. PRAEGER, *Publishers*

New York · Washington

BOOKS THAT MATTER

Published in the United States of America in 1968
by Frederick A. Praeger, Inc., Publishers
111 Fourth Avenue, New York, N.Y. 10003

Introduction © 1968 in London, England, by Robert
Conquest

Library of Congress Catalog Card Number: 68-17377

This book is Number 201 in the series
*Praeger Publications in Russian History and World
Communism*

Printed in Great Britain

Contents

Contents

Editor's Preface

Marx's definition of religion as 'the opium of the people' is one of the most widely known of his remarks. But in context, it will be seen that it does not carry the harsh and cynical tone which appears in that bare phrase:

'Religion is the sigh of the oppressed creature, the heart of a heartless world, the spirit of soulless stagnation. It is the *opium* of the people.'*

In fact, we can summarise this humane and sensitive passage by saying that in Marx's view those deprived of real satisfactions in the real world compensate themselves by inventing or accepting comforting fantasies.

Lenin held Marx's opinion in a far harsher and more hostile form. 'Religion is the opium of the people ... Religion is a kind of spiritual gin in which the slaves of capital drown their human shape and their claims to any decent life.'†

Any sort of religious attitude he denounced in the most bitter terms:

'Every religious idea, every idea of God, even flirting with the idea of God, is unutterable vileness ... vileness of the most dangerous kind, "contagion" of the most abominable kind. Millions of sins, filthy deeds, acts of violence and *physical* contagions ... are far less dangerous than the *subtle*, spiritual idea of a God decked out in the smartest "ideological" costumes. ... *Every* defence or justification of the idea of God, even the most refined, the best intentioned, is a justification of reaction.'‡

About all religious bodies he is equally uncompromising:

'All modern religions and Churches, all religious organisations, Marxism always regards as organs of *bourgeois* reaction serving to defend exploitation and to stupefy the working class.'§

* Marx and Engels, *Sochineniya*, Vol. 1, p. 385.
† Lenin, *Sochineniya*, Vol. 10, p. 66.
‡ Lenin, *Sochineniya*, Vol. 35, pp. 89–90 and 93.
§ Lenin, *Sochineniya*, Vol. 15, pp. 371–372.

[7]

Lenin's theory of morality was in any case incompatible with any teachings, religious or otherwise, which maintain the absolute nature of ethical standards: 'Our morality is completely subordinated to the interests of the class struggle of the proletariat. . . . Morality is that which serves to destroy the old exploiting society.' Therefore, 'we deny all morality that is drawn from some conception beyond men, beyond class. We say that it is a deception, . . . a fraud and a stultification of the minds of the workers and peasants in the interests of the landowners and capitalists.'*

Lenin saw the roots of religion as lying in economic exploitation: 'The social oppression of the toiling masses, their apparent complete helplessness before the blind forces of capitalism . . . that is the deepest contemporary root of religion.'†

Proceeding from his premise that 'the oppression of humanity by religion is only the product and reflection of the economic oppression within society',‡ the Communists originally held that in a society without 'hostile classes', without 'exploitation of man by man' there would be no religion. As the programme of the Soviet Communist Party, adopted in 1919, put it: 'The exercise of conscious planning in all the social and economic activities of the masses will bring with it the complete dying away of religious prejudices.'§

The process, however, was not expected to be automatic, and the tactical theory laid down was one of peaceful persuasion. The 1919 Party programme covers the methods to be used:

'The Party strives for the complete destruction of the ties between the exploiter classes and the organisation of religious propaganda; it furthers the actual liberation of the toiling masses from religious prejudices and organises the broadest scientific-educational and anti-religious propaganda.'

And there was a rider about the need to avoid offending the feelings of 'believers', because this would 'only lead to the strengthening of religious fanaticism'.¶

Lenin himself saw a need for tactical, outward compromise,

* Lenin, *Sochineniya*, Vol. 31, pp. 266–268.
† Lenin, *Sochineniya*, Vol. 15, pp. 374–375.
‡ Lenin, *Sochineniya*, Vol. 10, p. 68.
§ *KPSS v Rezolyutsiyakh*, Vol. 1, p. 420.
¶ *KPSS v Rezolyutsiyakh*, Vol. 1, pp. 420–421.

on the subject, even within the Party. Before he came to power he had written:

'Why do we not declare in our programme that we are atheists? Why do we not refuse Christians and those who believe in God admission to our Party? . . . Unity in the revolutionary struggle of the oppressed class for the creation of paradise on earth is more important to us than unity of opinion among the proletarians about a paradise in heaven. That is why we do not and must not proclaim our atheism in the programme; that is why we do not and must not forbid proletarians who still retain certain relics of the old superstitions to draw near our party.'*

He went further: 'We must not only admit but deliberately recruit into the party all workers who have preserved their belief in God.' He promised: 'We are unconditionally against the least offence to their religious convictions', but added: 'We recruit them in order to educate them in the spirit of our programme.'†

And the implications of this education are clear enough, as when he says, 'We demand that religion should be a private matter as far as the State is concerned, but under no circumstances can we regard religion as a private matter as far as our own party is concerned.'‡

I remember once having this tactic explained to me by a cynical Communist: 'First, you explain that a Christian can be a Communist. Later you explain that a Communist cannot be a Christian.' For, as Lenin put it '. . . The ideological struggle is not a private but a general party, proletarian matter.'§

Although the anti-religious campaign is accorded a good deal of theoretical importance, it has always been something of a sideline in practice, with more urgent problems clamouring for the Party's major attention. As a result, the cadres allotted to it seem to have been in the main thoroughly second-rate, people not thought suitable for more concrete work, and qualifying only by adequate fanaticism, and willingness to intrude. And the atheist argument in the Soviet Union is very often conducted in very low-grade terms. (As we shall see, one of the most frequently repeated points in this anti-

* Lenin, *Sochineniya*, Vol. 10, pp. 68–69.
† Lenin, *Sochineniya*, Vol. 15, pp. 377–378.
‡ Lenin, *Sochineniya*, Vol. 10, pp. 66–68.
§ Lenin, *loc cit.*

[9]

religious literature has been that the Sputniks have not discovered any god or heaven in the sky.)

Perhaps partly as a result of this, the provision that religion is to be combated by argument rather than by *force majeure* has never been adhered to. It is of course clear that the Communist style of rule gives great controversial advantages to the proponents of the official view. Thus, after a campaign of anti-religious propaganda in a given village, a vote would be taken on the closing down of the church. As with other voting in the Soviet Union, the official view had an excellent chance of prevailing. But in addition there has been considerable recourse to direct violence, and the arrest and persecution of the priesthood and laity.

The extent of pressures in the post-war period emerges in Alexander Solzhenitsyn's *A Day in the Life of Ivan Denisovich*, which makes it clear why the Baptists are sentenced: 'All they did was pray to God. And were they in anybody's way? They all got twenty-five years, because that's how it was now—twenty-five years for everybody.'

The combination of pressure and of indoctrination, in particular of the young, has had a considerable measure of success. A fair proportion of the younger generation is alienated from religion. But the expected collapse of religious belief has nevertheless not taken place, and in some respects it flourishes as strongly as before.

On Marx's view, religion will flourish in proportion to the unpleasantness of ordinary existence. When and if the truly Good Life for all, or the great majority, is established in the Soviet Union, a good Marxist might expect religion to die out. But it is clear that even now both material and spiritual conditions in the Soviet Union are not at the required level—being, indeed, in most respects far less satisfactory than those of the admittedly imperfect societies of the West. Moreover, the Soviet past was worse still, and might have been expected to establish religious habits of mind in many of those who suffered. Of the generation now in middle age, large numbers underwent senseless bereavement, an experience notoriously tending to turn many minds to religion. It is a curious sign of the persistence of religious feeling that in Russia's premier poet, Pasternak, life under the Soviets fortified rather than eroded it; and it is at least equally revelatory that Stalin's own daughter, brought up in an atheist conformity, turned from it to religion at the age of thirty-five. There are still frequent Soviet reports of the conversion to religion even of members of the intelligentsia—a fact that always gives grave offence to the Soviet Press, particularly in the case of medical students.

As in the time of the great slave empires, millenarian sects continually spring up: many of the tenets of the lesser groups more or less spontaneously arising are highly bizarre, as given in articles in the Soviet Press which occasionally expose them. In the labour camps, in particular, they secretly flourished. It is still frequently reported that those of the old labour camp areas which are now settled by released convicts are major haunts of religion, often in its most unyielding form. Jehovah's Witnesses, for example, are reported in Vorkuta and Karaganda. (It is significant that they were also found, in large numbers and unbroken, in the Nazi concentration camps.)

The main features of the campaign arise more or less equally with all the faiths of the Soviet Union, in accordance with Lenin's blanket condemnation. In this book, we examine the factual history and nature of the confrontation largely in connection with the Orthodox Church, which has been the largest-scale religious phenomenon the régime has faced.

Orthodoxy was the official religion of Imperial Russia and the Orthodox Church was subordinated to the Tsarist State, which ensured it a privileged position. On the eve of the First World War, the latest date for which official pre-revolutionary statistics are available, the Orthodox Church had a nominal membership of about 100,000,000. In its 67 dioceses it had 54,174 churches of all types (40,437 of them in the predominantly Russian dioceses), served by 50,105 priests and deacons. There were 1,025 monastic institutions housing 94,629 monks, nuns and novices. In addition to an annual State subsidy of tens of millions of roubles the Church possessed extensive resources of its own.* Its life under the Soviet régime adequately illustrates the typical and general conduct of the confrontation. But, in many instances, special measures have been taken with particular creeds, and we consider these separately.

While, in a sense, the attitude of the Soviet régime to religion is only one aspect of its attitude to all non-Communist thought, it is clear that the lines of conflict run at very basic

* *Vsepoddanneishi Otchet Ober-Prokurora*, pp. 4–7 and p. 67 of tables; Curtiss pp. 9–10.

levels—on the nature of life and death, of the universe and of ethical principle.

Needless to say, the progress of a conflict conducted in the terms explored in this book can not in itself strengthen or weaken the credibility in the abstract of either of the views concerned. It does, however, throw an important and interesting political, moral and intellectual light on recent Soviet history.

Acknowledgements are due to Messrs. I. I. Stepanov, M. Friedman and H. S. Murray, and to the late Walter Kolarz, for their invaluable collaboration or advice.

ROBERT CONQUEST

I

Religion in the USSR after the Revolution

The committee which elaborated the first constitution of the Russian Soviet Republic wrote into its draft the liberal formula: 'Religion is the private affair of citizens.' Lenin, however, rejected this formula and ordered its replacement by a provision guaranteeing 'freedom of religious and anti-religious propaganda'. This became Article 13 of the RSFSR Constitution of July 10, 1918.[1] It was a confrontation in which anti-religious propaganda was to be pursued with all the forces of the State and the Communist Party while religious propaganda was to be undertaken by Churches weakened, if not crippled, by discriminatory legislation.

This legislation had three features. Firstly, the Churches were deprived of material means and juridical existence. On December 4, 1917, all land was nationalised, including that of the churches and monasteries.[2] On January 23, 1918, Church and State were separated by a sweeping decree[3] which ordered the nationalisation without compensation of all Church-owned property: 'Churches and religious societies have no right to own property. They do not have the rights of juridical persons.'[4] The central or local authorities were, however, empowered to return to 'religious organisations' those 'buildings and objects that are needed for religious services'.[5] At the same time the legality of specifically ecclesiastical modes of organisation was placed in doubt. The official designation was 'ecclesiastical and religious societies' and these were made subject to the same laws and regulations as other societies and associations.[6] They were forbidden to 'levy obligatory collections or imposts' from their members in order to support themselves and they were not to 'coerce or punish' their members.[7]

Divine service was thus permitted to continue, but under

conditions of extreme hardship. Weak and disorganised 'religious groups' (as the parishes were officially designated) had to negotiate with the atheist State for the bare necessities which once obtained could, under the decree,[8] be only the property of individuals—and private property was often confiscated. Furthermore the groups were not allowed exclusive use of their buildings; for the Commissariat of Justice (in charge of 'religious affairs' until 1924) ordered that churches might be simultaneously used for secular, and often anti-religious, purposes such as courses of instruction, lectures, concerts, cinema shows, political meetings and popular dances.[9]

Secondly, priests and clerics were reduced to a socially inferior position. They were proclaimed 'servants of the bourgeoisie' and disfranchised (RSFSR Constitution of July 10, 1918, Article 65),[10] As disfranchised persons they received either no ration cards at all or cards of the lowest category; they were not allowed to belong to trade unions and so could not be employed by State enterprises; their children were barred from schools above the elementary grade; they had to pay higher rents for living quarters and higher rates of taxation.[11]

Thirdly, the Churches' influence on society, particularly in education, was destroyed. The decree of January 23, 1918, forbade religious instruction in State and public schools, and also in private schools where general subjects were taught. It was only permitted to 'study or teach religious subjects privately'.[12] This permission was restricted by a decree of June 13, 1921, which prohibited the religious instruction anywhere of groups of persons below the age of 18.[13]

The social influence of religion was further undermined by a decree of December 18, 1917, incorporated into the RSFSR Family Code of October 22, 1918, refusing legal recognition to church marriages and divorces, performed after the date of the decree.[14]

In addition to these hard but still oblique blows at the Churches a direct assault was made on the monasteries. The Commissariat of Justice ordered the 'painless but complete liquidation of the monasteries, as chief centres of the influence of the Churchmen'.[15] By 1920, 673 had been 'liquidated', their 2¼ million acres and 4,248,000,000 roubles confiscated, and their 84 factories, 436 dairy farms, 602 cattle farms, 1,112 apartment houses and 704 hostelries 'nationalised'.[16]

These measures met with considerable resistance and violence was used in carrying them out. Twenty-eight bishops and more than 1,000 priests of the Orthodox Church had perished in these conflicts by 1923.[17]

These 'necessary measures of a repressive character'[18] reached a climax in May, 1922. In February it had been decreed that objects of gold, silver and precious stones should be removed from the churches of all religions and handed over for famine relief.[19] This decree was enforced, often against bitter resistance; some 1,400 fights around churches were reported.[20]

Subsequently a direct assault was launched on the most prominent and influential churchmen, including the Patriarch, and an attempt was made to promote internal disruption by schism. The main blow in the direct assault was the trial in Moscow, from April 26 to May 6, of 54 Orthodox priests and laymen on charges of counter-revolution, i.e., agitation against the confiscation of Church treasures.[21] The Patriarch, called as a witness, declared it his duty to proclaim and obey canon law even where it might conflict with civil law.[22] His fate seemed sealed by the execution of five of the accused.[23] Three months later Metropolitan Veniamin of Petrograd and three co-defendants were executed for similar 'crimes'.[24] Kalinin, Chairman of the Soviets' Central Executive Committee, emphasised the magnitude and purpose of this terror by declaring that 'the heads of the Church have declared civil war against the government . . . there cannot and will not be mercy for those princes of the Church'.[25]

As early as March the official Press had referred approvingly to 'that more democratic part of the clergy that find within themselves some sort of common feeling with the suffering masses and protect it against the violence of the group of commanding church heads'.[26] There now appeared a group of 'progressive' priests whose motives are obscure but whose leaders, the Bishop Antonin and the Deacons Krasnitsky and Vvedensky, were ready to inform and testify against their spiritual superiors (at the Trials of the Fifty-Four[27] and of Metropolitan Veniamin[28]).

These men, styling themselves 'the Initiative Group of the Orthodox Church', on May 12 visited Patriarch Tikhon, then under close arrest, and browbeat him into renouncing his authority.[29] The same day the first issue appeared of their newly licensed journal Zhivaya Tserkov (The Living Church, a name soon applied to the schism itself). This contained a memorandum to the Central Executive Committee asking for the formation of a governmental 'All-Russian Committee for Affairs of the Orthodox Church' to organise all clerics and laymen 'who recognise the righteousness of the Russian social revolution and are loyal to the Soviet power'.[30]

On May 18 the 'Initiative Group' persuaded the Patriarch to entrust the administration of Church business to them 'temporarily'. Constituting themselves the 'Temporary Higher Church Administration' they took control of the entire administrative machinery.[31]

The State did all it could to advance the schism. It kept the Patriarch under arrest and threat of trial. It forcibly turned over many Church buildings to the 'Living Church'. With its assistance 84 bishops were expelled from their sees and more than 1,000 priests from their parishes to make room for the new organisation.[32]

In the 'Living Church' the Communists sought an organisation with which to destroy the ancient Orthodox Church. The 'Living Church' had little other purpose than to 'condemn' the activity of that Church and depose the Patriarch which it duly did at the *Sobor* or congress which it was permitted to summon in April, 1923,[33] Its governmental protectors themselves admitted that its programme was otherwise 'very modest'.[34]

The 'Living Church' was a failure; the Orthodox Church remained faithful to the Patriarch. 'Behind the Renovationist Movement [as it also styled itself] these turned out to be only small groups of supporters.'[35] So the Communists abandoned it; the Commissariats of Justice and Internal Affairs forbade any further administrative intervention in support of one cult or denomination against another.[36] The 'Living Church', torn by internal dissension, dwindled into insignificance.[37] The Government came to terms with the Patriarch. An indictment accusing him of 'dealings with foreign powers, counter-revolutionary work', etc., etc., had been published in April[38] and aroused indignation throughout Europe.[39] At the end of June it was announced that the Patriarch had acknowledged and abjured his hostility to the Soviet régime and asked the RSFSR Supreme Court to order his release. He was freed on June 25, 1923.[40] So ended the first period of the Communist attack on religion.

(b) 1923–1927

Intensive atheist propaganda became the order of the day. Specific directives were laid down at the 12th Congress of the

Communist Party in April, 1923. The Congress admitted that 'the deliberately rough methods which have often been practised both centrally and locally and the derision of articles of faith and worship instead of serious analysis and explanation do not accelerate but hinder the liberation of the toiling masses from religious prejudices'.[41]

The basic methods of 'profound systematic propaganda' prescribed by the Congress included:

(1) The publication of 'popular scientific' literature, particularly literature which would 'seriously elucidate the history and origin of religion', pamphlets and leaflets which would 'unmask the counter-revolutionary rôle of religion and the Church, especially the Russian Church as well as the physiognomy and real class nature of the various sects having influence over the popular masses';

(2) The organisation of 'mass anti-religious propaganda in the form of lively and comprehensible lectures';

(3) The training of party agitators and propagandists for the 'struggle against religion' in special courses and the organisation under party supervision of 'special anti-religious study circles and seminaries';

(4) The 'instruction in school of the toiling masses of town and country in the spirit of materialist natural science' and the 'liquidation of illiteracy'.[42]

A small beginning had already been made. A newspaper called *Bezbozhnik* (The Godless) had first appeared in Moscow in December, 1922,[43] and Christmas (celebrated in January in Russia) had been marked by an 'anti-Christmas carnival'; 'Within 10 days, 40 preliminary meetings were organised and the following themes were selected for the mock procession: the Performance of Miracles; the opening of Holy Shrines; the Immaculate Conception.'[44] Such disjointed efforts could not, however, satisfy the requirements of the party, so the correspondents and subscribers of *Bezbozhnik*, mainly party propagandists and agitators, were organised into a 'Society of Friends of the Paper *Bezbozhnik*'. This society held a congress in 1925 which decided to form a 'League of the Godless'.[45] Membership at first was small, numbering on January 1, 1926, 87,033, organised in 2,421 cells; by 1928 the number of cells had risen to 3,900, with 123,007 members.[46] Though ostensibly a 'voluntary social organisation', the League was openly stated to have been 'organised to assist the party by uniting all anti-religious propaganda workers under the general direction of the party'.[47] The chairman of its central Council and editor of *Bezbozhnik* was Emelyan Yaroslavsky, member of the Party Central Committee from 1921, secretary of the party's disciplinary Central Control Commission and member of the Central Executive Committee of the USSR from 1923.[48] Its secretary for many years was F. N. Oleshchuk, a veteran party member and collaborator with the Central Committee's Department of Propaganda and Agitation (Agitprop) of which he became a deputy director in the 1940s.[49] It was through this department that the Politburo's instructions were relayed to the League. A circular of the department instructed all party organisations to exercise systematic direction of the work of the 'cells'.[50]

The League devoted its main efforts to publications. Besides *Bezbozhnik* it put out *Antireligioznik* (The Anti-religious), a 'theoretico-methodological' monthly, a weekly *Bezbozhnik* for popular consumption, and two other periodicals, *Voinstvuyushchiy Atheism* (Militant Atheism) and *Derevensky Bezbozhnik* (The Village Godless), as well as equivalent publications in Ukrainian, Tatar, Georgian, Uzbek, Yiddish and other languages. The League also assisted in the publication and distribution of pamphlets and books, such as Yaroslavsky's *The Bible for Believers and Unbelievers* (in five volumes, Moscow, 1923–1925). It also opened and maintained anti-religious museums in some 40 cities.[51]

The League was not alone in the anti-religious field. The party took a direct hand through Agitprop and the local party organs; the Moscow Party Committee, for example, began pubishing in December, 1923, an anti-religious monthly, *Bezbozhnik u Stanka* (The Godless at the Machine), for 'the mass worker reader'. There were 70,000 copies per issue.

The Soviets, the Red Army and the trade unions were also drawn into the campaign. The Central Council of Trade Unions ordered the unions to integrate anti-religious activity with their club work, libraries, entertainments, etc. Clubs should be particularly active on religious holidays in order to keep the masses out of church.[52] Combined operations for training anti-religious personnel were in full swing by January 1, 1927, when there were 68 anti-religious seminaries and 15 reference centres for anti-religious workers.[53] The Red Army trained anti-religious personnel for rural work after demobilisation. In the summer of 1928 chairs for the study of religion were established in the Party's Communist Academy and the Institute of Red Professors.

Academic anti-religious instruction was begun in the universities. An 'anti-religious university' was opened in Moscow.[54]

In 1927 Stalin laid down the party 'line' on religion:

'The Party cannot be neutral towards religion, and it conducts anti-religious propaganda against all religious prejudices because it stands for science, whereas religious prejudices run counter to science, because all religion is the antithesis of science. . . . The party cannot be neutral towards the disseminators of religious prejudices, towards the reactionary clergy, who poison the minds of the labouring masses. Have we repressed the reactionary clergy? Yes, we have. The only unfortunate thing is that they have not yet been completely eliminated. Anti-religious propaganda is the means by which the elimination of the reactionary clergy will be completely carried through. Cases occur sometimes when certain members of the party hinder the full development of anti-religious propaganda. If such members are expelled it is a very good thing, because there is no room for such "Communists" in the ranks of our party.'[55]

Despite the predominant emphasis on propaganda 'rough' methods were not altogether abandoned. The 13th Party Congress in May, 1924, found it necessary to order 'the decisive liquidation of all attempts to struggle against religious prejudices by administrative methods such as the closing of churches, mosques, synagogues, prayer houses, etc'.[56] thus implying that such methods were still being used.

The possibilities for 'religious propaganda' were further reduced. On July 16, 1924, the teaching of religion in churches was prohibited.[57] On September 26, a decree on 'Religious Education of Minors' laid down that parents might give religious instruction to their children but not more than three children from other families could be present.[58]

Persecution of the Orthodox hierarchy also continued. Patriarch Tikhon died on April 7, 1925, naming Metropolitan Peter of Krutitsy as *locum tenens* until the election of a new Patriarch. But on December 25, 1925, the Metropolitan was arrested and in the summer of 1926 exiled to Siberia. He had, however, already decreed that if he were arrested Metropolitan Sergei of Nizhni Novgorod should be deputy *locum tenens*. Metropolitan Sergei was arrested early in 1926 and taken to Moscow for questioning. Released in March, he was rearrested on December 13, 1926. At that moment, of 11 hierarchs who had been nominated as *locum tenens* since the death of Tikhon, 10 were in prison or exile. But this devoted unity brought results. Early in 1927 Metropolitan Sergei succeeded in negotiating a *modus vivendi* with the State whereby legal recognition of the Orthodox Church was granted in return for assurances of the Church's loyalty and abstention from politics. In April the Metropolitan was released and confirmed as acting head of the Church.[59]

(c) 1928–1932

A critical year in the history of the USSR, 1928 saw the launching of Stalin's plans for forced industrialisation and compulsory collectivisation of agriculture. In such a situation an even more energetic campaign against religion was inevitable, for Stalin's plans could only be implemented by compulsion, which was certain to generate opposition. The Church was regarded as one of the centres around which such opposition would be centred; for the Church and its influence were still strong. It has been estimated that in 1928 the Orthodox Church still had about 39,000 churches.[60] Yaroslavsky reckoned that only some 10,000,000 (out of a population of 130,000,000) had broken with all religion.[61] And the Moscow Registry Office admitted that in 1928 57·8 per cent of all births and 65·7 per cent of all burials were marked by religious ceremonies; the percentage of religious marriages had, however, dropped from 21·1 in 1925 to 11·8 in 1928.[62]

The renewed attack on religion was launched on what Yaroslavsky called 'an extended front'. Direct suppression involved arrest of the clergy and mass closures of churches. Many bishops —and their successors—were arrested, most being sent to the notorious Solovetsky concentration camp on a group of islands in the White Sea. Thousands of priests were exiled or executed, many having been seized as hostages for the murder of local officials by peasants resisting collectivisation.[63] Many others, both priests and laymen, were penalised under articles entitled 'Violation of the Regulations Concerning the Separation of the Church from the State', contained in Chapter 4 of the Criminal Codex of the RSFSR which came into force on January 1, 1927. Up to one year's 'corrective labour' might be imposed for 'the teaching of religious beliefs to young children or minors in State or private educational institutions or schools', or 'in violation of the established rules' and also for 'the commission of deceitful acts for the purpose of inspiring superstition in the masses of the population with a view to deriving thereby any kind of profit whatsoever'. Up to six months' 'corrective labour' was the penalty for 'enforced collection of contributions' to religious organisations and for the assumption of administrative, judicial or any other legal functions of 'juridical persons' by religious organisations. Up to three months' 'corrective labour' was the punishment for the performance of 'religious rites' in State or 'social' establishments, 'and equally for the placing in these establishments of any religious images whatsoever'.

More menacing still were two articles in Chapter I, entitled 'State Crimes'. Article 58/10 stipulated that for propaganda or agitation calling for 'the overthrow, undermining or weakening' of the Soviet régime, or the distribution, preparation or retention of literature with such content, if use was made of 'the religious prejudices of the masses' the penalty might range from execution to not less than three years' imprisonment under mitigating circumstances. Article 59/7 stipulated a penalty of up to two years' imprisonment for propaganda or agitation directed to stirring up religious hatred or dissension, or for distributing, preparing or retaining literature for this purpose.[64]

In April, 1929, the Komsomol newspaper called for the confiscation and melting down of church bells.[65] Afterwards 'popular demands' for the removal of bells were reported from all over the country and by the end of the year the bells had gone from 'hundreds of villages and a number of towns', of which Stalingrad (now Volgograd) was one of the first.[66] The removal of bells from a church was often the prelude to its closure—again allegedly to meet 'popular demands'. In 1929 alone, 1,440 churches were closed.[67] The way in which it was done has been described by a foreigner in the USSR at the time:

'In thousands of villages where wholesale collectivisation of farming was going on, local Communists or members of the Young Communist League called meetings which voted over the heads of the congregations to demolish the churches, melt down the bells, or turn church buildings into granaries, schools, theatres. . . . A semblance of popular consent was thus created. But when brigades arrived to remove the bells and icons, they sometimes found believers armed with sticks and pitchforks to defend their church. The troops, in many instances, were summoned to crush these riots and the ringleaders found themselves quickly enough in prison or before the firing squad.'[68]

Another sector of the 'extended front' covered measures to undermine those religious organisations which survived the direct attack. Perhaps the most enduring of these measures was the law of April 8, 1929, 'Concerning Religious Associations',[69]

[21]

dealing with the legal position of religious organisations. This decree, still in force, codified earlier regulations. It laid down that all 'cults' must be registered as 'religious societies or groups of believers', no citizen being allowed to belong to more than one society or group.[70] 'Activities' might not begin until after registration with 'the appropriate authority'[71] which could refuse registration[72] or 'remove' individuals from membership of the 'executive organ' of the 'society' or 'group'.[73] The decree also introduced new restrictions. Religious organisations were forbidden to establish mutual assistance funds, co-operatives or unions of producers; to extend material aid to their members; 'to organise special prayer or other meetings for children, youths or women, or to organise general bible, literary, handicraft, working, religious study or other meetings, groups, circles or branches, to organise excursions or children's playgrounds, or to open libraries or reading rooms, or to organise sanatoria or medical aid'.[74] As an official commentator put it: 'The activities of all religious associations were reduced to the performance of the cult. Activities exceeding the limits whereby this need was satisfied were no longer permitted.'[75]

Article 18 of the decree stated: 'The teaching of any religious faith whatsoever is not allowed in State, social or private educational institutions.' According to the same commentator, this annulled the right of parents to have their children given religious instruction by the priest; only parents might teach their children religion.[76] The Commissariat of Internal Affairs was, however, empowered to license the opening of special theological courses for people over 17 years of age.[77]

Since the provisions of Article 18 conflicted with the constitutional right of 'religious propaganda' an amendment was adopted on May 22, 1929, whereby 'freedom of religious worship and anti-religious propaganda' was substituted for 'freedom of religious and anti-religious propaganda'.[78] This meant, the commentator explained, that the Constitution no longer permitted either 'the winning of new groups of the workers, especially children, as adherents of religion', or 'any kind of propaganda on the part of the Churches and religious persons'.[79]

New efforts were made to make the position of ministers as nearly intolerable as possible. The April decree[80] limited the activity of a priest to the area of his parish. His material situation was made increasingly difficult. At the beginning of 1930 it was claimed that 'the taxation policy of the Soviet régime is

[22]

striking the pockets of the servitors of religious cults especially painfully'.[81] From 1928 members of the clergy were made to pay higher rents.[82] In January, 1930, it was intimated that all disfranchised persons, among them the clergy, were to be expelled from all nationalised and municipally-owned housing.[83] They met difficulties in obtaining food and other necessities. In 1930 the Central Co-operative Union forbade the provisioning of disfranchised persons (but not their children) without prior payment of a special deposit.[84]

The 'extended front' included not only these repressive measures but also others specifically designed to inculcate atheism. Particular attention was paid to the schools. In 1925 the State School Council in a letter on methods entitled 'Non-religious Education in the School' had observed that 'special implanting of anti-religiousness in the soul of the child is not needed'.[85] But in the spring of 1927 the League of Godless began campaigning for more energetic anti-religious efforts in schools and by mid-1928 the term 'non-religious education' was dropped. Early in 1929 the Commissariat of Education issued a letter on methods of anti-religious instruction.[86]

The 8th Congress of the Komsomol in 1928 ordered intensification of anti-religious work. Young Communists were instructed to unmask the clergy as defenders of the prosperous peasants, to train as anti-religious volunteers and to carry on atheistic propaganda and agitation. These Komsomol activities became particularly marked in 1929.[87] At a conference of the Godless League in June, 1929, the Komsomol representatives proposed that trade unionists should be compelled to abandon membership of religious associations. Their proposal was rejected on the grounds that it would in fact reinforce religious sentiments.[88]

In March, 1929, the 8th Congress of Trade Unions stressed the anti-religious struggle as an important part of trade union activity. A circular ordered extended anti-religious work in union clubs and libraries and the training of atheists in the courses of the Godless League.[89] A few months later the All-Union Central Council of Trade Unions (AUCCTU) issued an explanation of the decree of August 26 instituting the continuous work week and entailing the staggering of workers' weekly rest days. While the primary object was economic the Council explained that by eliminating general Sunday holidays and saints' days the measure would facilitate 'a more successful struggle against religion'.[90]

The intensity of the anti-religious campaign was reflected in a much greater recruitment into the League of the Godless. By January 1, 1929, it had 8,928 cells with 465,498 members.[91] A year later there were 35,000 cells with 2,000,000 members.[92] At its second congress in 1929 the League changed its name, significantly, to 'League of Militant Godless of the USSR'[93] and stepped up its activities. Anti-Easter and anti-Christmas campaigns were put on each year. The anti-Christmas campaign in January, 1930, was reported as a great success, with ceremonial burnings of icons and demands for the closing of churches.[94] In one district over 100 out of 300 churches were closed during the campaign.[95] A year earlier *Pravda* had condemned all outward signs of Christmas such as the sale of Christmas trees, decoration of stores with Christmas emblems and the preparation of religious supplies by State enterprises.[96]

The violence of these efforts proved self-defeating. Many people were shocked by the harsh, coercive methods employed, while believers were only confirmed in their faith. In February, 1930, Metropolitan Sergei reported that the Orthodox Church alone still had 30,000 parishes, 163 bishops and tens of millions of believers.[97]

These considerations would not in themselves have made Stalin moderate the campaign. It was the combined opposition to atheism and collectivisation which decided him to reduce the pressure. The turning point was marked by his article 'Dizzy with Success' in *Pravda* of March 2, 1930, in which he denounced excesses in the collectivisation drive.[98] A fortnight later the Central Committee adopted a resolution 'On the Struggle against Distortions of the Party Line in the Kolkhoz Movement' which admitted:

'The Central Committee considers it necessary to note completely inadmissible distortion of the Party line in the sphere of struggle against religious prejudices. . . . We have in mind the *administrative* closing of churches without the consent of the majority of the village, which generally leads to the strengthening of religious prejudices.'

All Party Committees were ordered:

'Decisively to *end* the practice of closing churches in an administrative manner fictitiously disguised as the public and voluntary wish of the population.'[99]

On March 23, the Presidium of the Central Executive Committee ordered 'the unconditional elimination' of excessive discrimination against the disfranchised, including the clergy, 'such as expulsion from their homes and their towns; wholesale deprivation of medical aid; prohibition of building; expulsion of their children from schools'.[100]

For the remainder of the First Five-Year Plan period (to 1932) the attack on religion continued, though rather less violently and with a great deal less enthusiasm. According to Yaroslavsky, many Godless misinterpreted the Central Committee's decree of March, 1930, as meaning that atheistic activity was no longer wanted.[101] In fact, he insisted, the need for able and effective anti-religious propaganda was as great as ever.[102]

The falling-off of the anti-religious effort was reflected in the failure of the Godless Five-Year Plan of recruitment whereby the membership was to reach 4,000,000 by the end of 1930, 7,000,000 by the end of 1931 and 17,000,000 by the end of 1933.[103] In fact by May, 1932, membership totalled only 5,673,000.[104] Nevertheless, optimistic predictions of 10,000,000 members by 1934 and 22,000,000 by 1937 were made.[105]

From 1930 a new emphasis was discernible in the work of the League. Yaroslavsky laid down that its efforts must be 'subordinated ... to the problems of Socialist construction'.[106] A major objective was the creation of Godless collective farms, the sowing of 'Godless hectares'.[107] In industry there were to be organised Godless factories and shops and 'Godless shock-brigades' combining anti-religious work with intensive production efforts. By July, 1931, there were some 3,200 such brigades demonstrating the thesis that 'anti-religion has a productional significance'.[108]

The anti-Easter and anti-Christmas campaigns continued with special emphasis on reducing absenteeism on religious holidays. Such absenteeism was also one reason for the decree of November 15, 1932,[109] whereby one day's unauthorised absence from work became punishable by confiscation of food and other ration cards and deprivation of the right to use the housing facilities of the enterprise concerned.

The number of two-year evening 'workers' anti-religious universities' in major cities grew from 44 in 1930 to 81 in 1931, and three 'peasants' anti-religious universities were established'.[110] There were also less ambitious courses in atheism; by 1933 there were 5,020 elementary courses with 144,161 students and 255 secondary courses with 4,135 students.[111] Anti-religious museums, usually in former churches and monasteries, reached a total of 44 in 1930. The previous year 263,880 people visited the Central Anti-Religious Museum in Moscow.[112] In 1932 an important new museum was opened in the Kazan Cathedral in Leningrad.[113] There was a proliferation of anti-religious publications. By 1930, 20 atheist periodicals were being published compared with four in 1925. The average monthly circulation of the newspaper *Bezbozhnik* was boosted from 63,100 in 1928 to 473,000 in 1931.[114]

The issue of non-periodical anti-religious literature was increased from 700,000 printed sheets in 1927 to 50,000,000 (800,000,000 pages) in 1930[115] In the decade 1922–32 about 40,000,000 copies of atheist books and pamphlets were issued, including the *Workers' Anti-Religious Textbook* (sixth edition of 100,000 copies in 1931) and the *Peasants' Anti-Religious Textbook* (sixth edition of 200,000 copies in 1931).[116]

The position of ministers of all religions continued to be difficult, and was aggravated by the introduction in December, 1932, of the internal passport system 'for the purpose of relieving inhabited localities of persons ... not occupied in socially useful work'.[117]

Churches continued to be closed. Moscow's pre-revolutionary 460 Orthodox churches were reduced by January 1, 1930, to 224, though the city's population had increased by almost half.[118] By January, 1933, the city had only 140 places of worship of which about 100 were Orthodox.[119] Elsewhere churches were eliminated altogether. For instance Kargopol, which had 23 churches in 1917, by 1932 had 'no churches with their tiresome bell-ringing'.[120]

(d) 1933–1937

A period of relaxation followed the rigours of the First Five-Year Plan. At first there was little change in the position of the Churches. The priests remained disfranchised and subject to deprivations which included the prohibition of university education for their children[121] and discriminatory taxation.[122] But with the 'victory of Socialism along the whole front', proclaimed at the 17th Party Congress (January, 1934) and the subsequent emphasis on 'Soviet Socialist democracy', the position improved.

Early in 1936 children of non-working parents were admitted to higher educational establishments.[123] The new Soviet Constitution adopted in December of the same year and still in force abolished all distinction between 'working' and 'non-working' persons. All the rights of citizenship, including the franchise, were given to all 'irrespective of race and national origin, religious profession, educational standing', etc.[124] But 'religious propaganda' remained banned: 'With the aim of securing freedom of conscience for citizens, the Church in the USSR is separated from the State and the school from the Church. Freedom of religious worship and freedom of anti-religious propaganda is recognised for all citizens.'[125]

Under these conditions the campaign to propagate atheism lost momentum. As early as December, 1932, a Godless conference was told: 'We know tens of Godless kolkhozes which in 1930–31 worked quite well on the anti-religious front, but with the end of 1931 and the beginning of 1932 complete collapse set in.'[126] The newspaper *Bezbozhnik* was wound up in 1934, while the circulation of the two leading Godless monthlies dropped sharply.[127] In 1933 the number of 'anti-religious universities' fell to 27.[128] The number of anti-religious museums fell to about 30 while the annual attendance at the Central Anti-Religious Museum in Moscow slumped to 157,000 people.[129]

In 1935, though he claimed that the number of those who 'have broken or are breaking with religion' amounted to 50,000,000, 'if not more',[130] Yaroslavsky admitted the continued existence of religious organisations with influence 'over tens of millions of working people'.[131] The next year he declared that 'ministers of cults of all confessions and ranks' numbered about 100,000.[132]

Anti-Easter and anti-Christmas carnivals came gradually to an end. At Christmas, 1935, the instigators of campaigns in Sverdlovsk and Vologda were censured; people were once again allowed to light Christmas trees and the State stores sold the traditional goods.[133] When in April, 1937, a mass campaign for the closing of churches was launched in the Vologda province it was forbidden as likely to embitter believers and fortify their convictions.[134]

(e) MID-1937–MID-1941

In the middle of 1937 the attack on the Churches suddenly flared up again. This was probably inevitable in the atmosphere of the purges taking place at that time. But there seem to have been two specific reasons. The first was the evidence of the

[27]

census of January 6, 1937, which required the listing of citizens over the age of 15 as believers or non-believers, with their denomination.[135] Allegedly because 'enemies of the people penetrated into the preparation and conduct of the census', its results were condemned by the Government as 'defective' and never published.[136] It was widely believed that the census had shown an unexpectedly large number of believers. This belief was borne out by the omission of all questions about religion from the new census of January 17, 1939.[137]

The second reason was the improvement in the position of the clergy, as the result of the 1936 Constitution. The granting of full citizenship rights, the Godless leaders maintained, would encourage the clergy to become more active.[138] It was further alleged: 'Seeking to pervert the true sense of the Stalin Constitution, the religious assert that the new Constitution recognises the usefulness of religion and religious organisations and that this testifies to the weakness of the Soviet régime and to a change in the attitude of the Communist Party towards religion.'[139] Matters came to a head over the election to the USSR Supreme Soviet, the successor of the Central Executive Committee. These elections took place on December 12, 1937, but were preceded by a preparatory campaign beginning with the adoption in July of 'Regulations for the Elections to the Supreme Soviet of the USSR'.[140] Echoing the Constitution, the regulations established that all citizens over the age of 17, except the insane and persons disfranchised by court order, 'have the right to take part in the election of deputies and to be elected to the Supreme Soviet'.[141] The right to propose candidates was granted to Communist Party organisations, trade unions, cooperatives, youth organisations, cultural societies and 'other organisations registered in the legally established manner'.[142] The clergy and believers inferred that their organisations qualified for this right and that the religious might be proposed and elected to the Supreme Soviet. The Soviet rulers had overlooked this development and so had openly to contravene their own electoral regulations. 'It was necessary', it was said, 'to give a decisive rebuff to the attempts of the priesthood to spread lying fabrications to the effect that religious organisations... have the constitutional right to put forward their own candidates.'[143]

In November, on the eve of the elections, groups of churchmen, including bishops, were arrested all over the Soviet Union on charges of organising espionage and sabotage in the interests

[28]

of Germany and Japan, and even of plotting the assassination of Soviet leaders.[144] This attack coincided with the climax of the terror carried out by Ezhov, Commissar of Internal Affairs. A major trial of churchmen, including a bishop, 12 priests and three deacons, was staged at Orel in the early summer. This 'gang of malicious enemies of the toilers of the USSR' had 'aimed at the strengthening . . . of the Church as a legalised institution for counter-revolutionary work. . . . Thus they wanted to take advantage of Article 124 of the Stalin Constitution.' Among the acts cited in support of the charge of counter-revolution were: attracting young people to the Church; publishing a prayer in Old Slavonic; holding general confessions; recommending priests banished from cities to go to the villages; urging people to petition for the re-opening of churches; baptising children of school age; hearing confession in the priest's home.[145]

A similar trial was publicised in February, 1938,[146] Oleshchuk gave the following account of it:

'In the Gorki province the organs of the NKVD unmasked a great nest of spies and diversionists hiding under the flag of religion. The organisation was headed by Metropolitan Feofan Tulyakov of Gorki, Bishop Korobov of Vetluga, Bishop Purlevsky of Sergach. . . . Bishop Korobov declared under investigation that the aim of this organisation, directed by the Moscow Centre, was anti-Soviet activity, finding expression in the collection of information about the condition of the collective farms and the morale and political mood of the collective farmers, in the destruction of the collective farms by incendiarism of the property of collective farms and rural activists, in the conducting of counter-revolutionary propaganda for an exodus from the collective farms, in the dissemination among the populace of provocatory rumours about imminent war and the ruin of the Soviet régime, in the dissemination of slanders about the leaders of the Party and the Soviet Government, in the conducting of agitation among believers for the opening of previously closed churches.'[347]

Once a clergyman had been arrested as a 'traitor' the church was often closed. In this way the number of Orthodox churches was reduced by 1939 to 20,000.[148] At the same time efforts to spread atheism were revived. The official signal was given in May, 1937, by *Pravda*. Condemning the 'rotten theory' that Soviet economic development was such that religion could be left to die a natural death, *Pravda* complained that the trade unions had not issued an order on anti-religious propaganda for six years; the Commissariat of Education had liquidated the anti-religious departments in higher educational establishments and 'is closing the anti-religious museums'; the Komsomol had failed to carry out its anti-religious programme; and the League of Militant Godless had been working 'exceedingly badly'. *Pravda* admitted that repressive anti-religious methods were still being used and ordered an increase in atheist propaganda:

'Our organisations, instead of patiently and firmly explaining to the masses the evils of religious obscurantism, are willing to relegate the whole struggle against religious prejudices to the sphere of administrative measures, closing places of worship without the consent of the citizens, and occasionally turning people out of work simply because they are believers. These zealous "administrators" fail to realise that this kind of "struggle" can only drive religion underground and hinder the genuine struggle against it. . . . It must be clearly understood that the believer is not an enemy of the Soviet régime, and that religious prejudices must be fought by an extensive anti-religious propaganda, not by high-handed administrative measures.'[149]

Appropriate steps were taken. The League of Militant Godless was resuscitated. In 1940 some 160,000 people were attending anti-religious courses and 239,000 atheistic lectures were delivered to 10,755,000 people.[150] The anti-religious museums were revived and their number increased to 47 by 1941.[151] Publishing activities were expanded. The newspaper *Bezbozhnik* resumed publication in 1938,[152] Particular attention was devoted to the schools. Young Pioneers were instructed to ridicule children who wore crosses or prayed to God.[153]

In contrast the Soviet leaders had in 1939 called off their third direct assault on the Churches. In June, 1940, the uniform seven-day week was readopted with Sunday as the day of rest.[154] It was thus recognised that the Lord's Day was still the generally accepted weekly rest day.

By 1941 the wheel had turned full circle three times. Thrice the Soviet leaders had tried to eliminate religion by persecution. Thrice they had failed. Now for the third time the emphasis shifted to anti-religious propaganda. However, the involvement of the USSR in the Second World War broke the cycle; the status of religion was to change rapidly.

SOURCES

1. Gurvich, pp. 79–80, RSFSR *Laws*, 1918, 51; 582, art. 13.
2. *RSFSR, Laws*, 1917, 1: 3.
3. *RSFSR Laws*, 1918, 18: 263.

4. *Ibid.*, art. 12.
5. *Ibid.*, art. 13.
6. *Ibid.*, art. 10.
7. *Ibid.*, art. 11.
8. *Ibid.*, art. 12.
9. Gidulyanov, 1926 edn., p. 654.
10. *RSFSR Laws*, 1918, 51: 582, art. 65.
11. Timasheff, pp. 26–27.
12. *RSFSR, Laws*, 1918, 18: 263, art. 9.
13. Gidulyanov, 1926 edn., p. 168.
14. *RSFSR Laws*, 1917, 11: 160; 1918; 76–77: 818, art. 52.
15. *Revolyutsiya i Tserkov*, 1920, No. 9–12, p. 83.
16. Oleshchuk, *Borba Tserkvi Protiv Naroda*, p. 22.
17. Timasheff, p. 54.
18. *B.S.E.*, 1st edn., Vol. on USSR, p. 1778.
19. *Izvestiya*, February 26, 1922.
20. *Pravda*, April 20, 1922.
21. *Izvestiya*, April 28, 1922.
22. *Izvestiya*, May 6, 1922.
23. *Izvestiya*, June 1, 1922.
24. *Izvestiya*, August 13, 1922.
25. *Izvestiya*, August 6, 1922.
26. *Izvestiya*, March 26, 1922.
27. *Izvestiya*, May 3, 1922.
28. *Izvestiya*, August 13, 1922.
29. *Pravda, Izvestiya*, May 17, 1922.
30. *Zhivaya Tserkov*, 1922, No. 1, p. 10.
31. *Pravda, Izvestiya*, May 21, 1922.
32. McCullagh, p. XVII.
33. *B.S.E.*, 1st edn., Vol. 42, p. 508.
34. *Ibid.*, Vol. 23, p. 670.
35. *Ibid.*, p. 671.
36. Gidulyanov, 1924 edn., p. 379.
37. Curtiss, p. 142.
38. *Izvestiya*, April 6, 1923.
39. Timasheff, p. 33.
40. *Izvestiya*, June 27, 1923.
41. *KPSS v Rezolyutsiyakh*, Vol. I, p. 744.
42. *Ibid.*, pp. 744–745.
43. *B.S.E.*, 2nd edn., Vol. 4, p. 380.
44. *Izvestiya*, January 10, 1923.
45. *B.S.E.*, 1st edn., Vol. 52, p. 334.
46. *Antireligioznik*, 1929, No. 6, p. 112.
47. *B.S.E.*, 1st edn., Vol. 3, p. 67.
48. *Ibid.*, Vol. 65, p. 780.
49. *Pravda*, January 4, 1945.
50. *Antireligioznik*, 1927, No. 10, p. 128.
51. *B.S.E.*, 1st edn., Vol. 52, p. 335; Curtiss, p. 210.
52. Orleansky, pp. 51–53.
53. Enisherlov, p. 375.
54. *Ibid.*, pp. 376–377, 328.
55. Stalin, *Works*, Vol. 10, pp. 138–139.
56. *KPSS v Rezolyutsiyakh*, Vol. II, p. 53.
57. Gidulyanov, 1926 edn., p. 373.
58. *Ibid.*, p. 374.
59. Curtiss, pp. 175–185.
60. *Ibid.*, p. 223.
61. Yaroslavsky, *Razvernutym Frontom*, pp. 8–9.
62. *Antireligioznik*, 1929, No. 6, pp. 89–91.
63. Timasheff, pp. 39–40.
64. *Ugolovny Kodeks* RSFSR, pp. 41, 20, 23.
65. *Komsomolskaya Pravda*, April 7, 1929.
66. *Antireligioznik*, 1930, No. 2, pp. 12–22.
67. *Ibid.*, No. 3.
68. Lyons, pp. 212–213.

69. *RSFSR Laws*, 1929, 35: 353.
70. *Ibid.*, art. 2.
71. *Ibid.*, art. 4.
72. *Ibid.*, art. 7.
73. *Ibid.*, art. 14.
74. *Ibid.*, art. 17.
75. Orleansky, p. 11.
76. *Ibid.*
77. *RSFSR Laws*, 1929, 35: 353, art. 18.
78. *Konstitutsii Soyuza SSR*, p. 22.
79. Orleansky, p. 47.
80. *RSFSR Laws*, 1929, 35: 353, art. 19.
81. *Antireligioznik*, 1930, No. 1, p. 5.
82. Orleansky, p. 57.
83. *Pravda*, January 3, 1930.
84. *Izvestiya*, June 6, 1930.
85. Enisherlov, pp. 289–290. 329–330.
86. *Ibid.*, pp. 291–295.
87. *Ibid.*, pp. 309–310.
88. Timasheff, p. 42.
89. Orleansky, pp. 53–55.
90. *Ibid.*, p. 134.
91. Enisherlov, pp. 344–345.
92. *Antireligioznik*, 1931, No. 1, p. 40.
93. *B.S.E.*, 1st edn., Vol. 52, p. 335.
94. *Pravda, Izvestiya*, January 8, 1930; *Antireligioznik*, 1930, No. 3, pp. 95–97.
95. *Antireligioznik*, 1930, No. 3, p. 47.
96. *Pravda*, December 25, 1928.
97. *Izvestiya*, February 19, 1930.
98. Stalin, *Problems of Leninism*, pp. 419–425.
99. *KPSS v Rezolyutsiyakh*, Vol. II, pp. 670–671.
100. *Izvestiya*, March 23, 1930.
101. *Pravda*, June 24, 1930.
102. *Antireligioznik*, 1932, No. 19–20, p. 11.
103. *Antireligioznik*, 1930, No. 4, p. 3.
104. Enisherlov, p. 347.
105. *Ibid.*, p. 352.
106. *Antireligioznik*, 1930, No. 3, p. 10.
107. *Pod Znamenem Marksizma*, 1931, No. 3, pp. 33–35.
108. *Antireligioznik*, 1931, No. 7, p. 3.
109. *USSR Law*, 1932, 78: 475.
110. *Antireligioznik*, 1931, No. 4, pp. 43–50.
111. *Antireligioznik*, 1933, No. 4, p. 38.
112. *Pod Znamenem Marksizma*, 1930, No. 3, p. 51.
113. *Pravda*, February 18, 1932.
114. Enisherlov, p. 395.
115. *Pod Znamenem Marksizma*, 1931, No. 3, p. 51.
116. Enisherlov, pp. 391–393.
117. *USSR Laws*, 1932, 84: 516.
118. *Antireligioznik*, 1930, No. 8–9, p. 101.
119. *Antireligioznik*, 1933, No. 3, p. 14.
120. *Derevensky Bezbozhnik*, 1932, No. 14.
121. *RSFSR Laws*, 1934, 36: 226, art. 15; *USSR Laws*, 1934, 13: 87b, art. 41.
122. *USSR Laws*, 1934, 27: 211b, art. 19.
123. *USSR Laws*, 1936, 1: 2.
124. Article 135; *O Konstitutsii Soyuza SSR*, p. 53.
125. Article 124; *ibid.*, p. 52.
126. *Antireligioznik*, 1933, No. 2, p. 27.
127. Anderson, op. cit., p. 13.
128. *Antireligioznik*, 1933, No. 4, p. 38.
129. *Antireligioznik*, 1936, No. 2, p. 27.

130. *Antireligioznik*, 1935, No. 4, p. 11.
131. *Antireligioznik*, No. 6, p. 4.
132. Yaroslavsky, *Stalinskaya Konstitutsiya Vopros o Religii*, p. 14.
133. Timasheff, pp. 46–47.
134. *Antireligioznik*, 1937, No. 5.
135. *USSR Laws*, 1936, 25: 237, 25: 238, art. 4.
136. Podyachikh, p. 12; *USSR Laws*, 1937, 65: 292.
137. *USSR Laws*, 1938, 35: 211.
138. *Bolshevik*, 1938, No. 16, pp. 35–37; *Izvestiya*, July 3, 1937.
139. Oleshchuk, op. cit., p. 76.
140. *O Konstitutsii Soyuza SSR*, pp. 57–70.
141. Article 2; *ibid.*, p. 57.
142. Article 56; *ibid.*, p. 64.
143. Oleshchuk, op. cit., p. 78.
144. Timasheff, p. 50.
145. *Bezbozhnik*, 1937, No. 7; for a translation of this report see Anderson, *People, Church and State in Modern Russia*, pp. 112–115.
146. *Izvestiya*, February 8, 1938; *Antireligioznik*, 1938, No. 3, pp. 7–8.
147. Oleshchuk, op. cit., pp. 85–86.
148. *Antireligioznik*, 1939, No. 6, p. 5.
149. *Pravda*, May 7, 1937.
150. *Antireligioznik*, 1941, No. 5, pp. 1–2.
151. *Ibid.*, p. 7.
152. *Pravda*, January 24, 1941.
153. *Komsomolskaya Pravda*, March 27, 1938.
154. *Vedomosti Verkhovnogo Soveta SSSR*, 1940, No. 20.

II

Religion During and After the
Second World War

(a) 1941–1945

In mid-summer, 1941, there were in the USSR 8,338 houses of prayer, about 30,000 registered religious communities and 58,442 ministers of religion. The Orthodox Church had only 4,225 churches, 37 monasteries, 28 Metropolitans and bishops, 5,665 priests and 3,100 deacons and sacristans.[1]

On June 22, the day of the German invasion, while Stalin remained silent, Metropolitan Sergei sent a message to all Orthodox parishes, reminding the faithful of the patriotic feats of their ancestors and declaring:

'Our Orthodox Church has always shared the fate of the people. It has always borne their trials and cherished their successes. It will not desert the people now. . . . The Church of Christ blesses all the Orthodox defending the sacred frontiers of our Motherland. The Lord will grant us victory.'[2]

This example was 'immediately followed by the leaders of almost all the other Churches and religious associations in the USSR'.[3]

On June 26 Metropolitan Sergei held a special service of prayer for the victory of the Soviet troops. It was the duty of all to defend the Motherland, he declared.[4]

Fighting for their lives, the Soviet leaders could not refuse such support. Anti-religious propaganda ceased.

On February 23, 1942, the Orthodox Churches and clergy of Moscow gave 1,500,000 roubles to the Red Army Fund.[5] In January, 1943, Metropolitan Sergei launched a campaign for contributions towards a 'Dmitri Donskoi' tank column.[6] On March 23, 1944, the Orthodox clergy of Moscow gave a further 1,000,000 roubles to build aircraft.[7] In all, during the war, the Orthodox Church contributed to the national defence more than 300,000,000 roubles.[8]

At the same time the Churches did much to bolster national morale and exhorted the populace to remain loyal to, and execute the policies of, the Soviet Government. Thus in January, 1942, Metropolitan Sergei published a message to people in German-occupied areas, warning them against purchasing well-being 'by treason to Church and Motherland'.[9] In June, in a message 'To the Whole Church' he paid tribute to the guerrillas and called for all possible support for them.[10] At Christmas, he encouraged the people of the occupied areas: 'Endure yet a little while . . . and once more light will shine upon you.'[11]

To the unstinted support of the Churches the Soviet leaders reacted with an attitude of cordiality in striking contrast to their former hostility. At Easter, 1942, the curfew was lifted in Moscow, so that the religious might attend midnight services.[12] In November, Metropolitan Nikolai of Kiev and Galicia was appointed to the Extraordinary State Commission for investigating German atrocities[13]—the first State appointment held by an ecclesiastic since the Revolution.

On September 4, 1943, an unprecedented event took place. Stalin and Molotov received Metropolitans Sergei, Aleksei and Nikolai in the Kremlin. This meeting sealed the *rapprochement* between the Orthodox Church and the State. Stalin gave permission for the calling, at long last, of a *Sobor* (Council) of bishops to elect a Patriarch and a Synod to assist him.[14]

On September 8 the *Sobor*, consisting of 19 bishops, met in Moscow to adopt unanimously a message of thanks to the Government for its solicitude, and another of exhortation to the Christians of the whole world to unite against Hitlerism; it elected Metropolitan Sergei as Patriarch of Moscow and All Russia and chose a Holy Synod.[15]

On September 12 the monthly *Journal of the Moscow Patriarchate* began publication. In October the relationship between the atheist State and the Orthodox Church was given administrative shape. The Council of People's Commissars of the USSR, it was reported, had decreed the establishment, as an adjunct to itself, of a Council for the Affairs of the Russian Orthodox Church 'to maintain liaison between the Government of the USSR and the Patriarch of Moscow and All Russia on questions of the Russian Orthodox Church requiring decision by the Government of the USSR'.[16] The Council, headed by G. G. Karpov, consisted of five members.

In July, 1944, the formation of a Council for the Affairs of

Religious Cults, headed by I. V. Polyansky, to perform the same functions in relation to the 'Armenian-Gregorian, Old Believer, Catholic, Graeco-Catholic and Lutheran Churches, the Muslim, Jewish and Buddhist creeds and sectarian organisations' was briefly reported.[17] The decrees setting up these councils were never themselves published, but a description of their organisation and functions has been given in the *Bolshaya Sovetskaya Entsiklopediya*. They are 'consultative organs of the Government,' and no representatives of religious bodies enter into their composition. They have their 'plenipotentiaries' attached to the Councils of Ministers of Union and Autonomous Republics and to the Executive Committees of *Krai* and *Oblast* Soviets. Their basic functions include:

(1) preparatory consideration for subsequent submission to the Government of such questions raised by religious bodies as require governmental decision ('the provision of buildings for purposes of worship, instruction, etc., the issue of materials, the provision of printing facilities, etc.');

(2) drafting for submission to the Government of laws and decrees relative to religious associations and of instructions for their application;

(3) supervision of the 'correct and timely' execution of governmental laws and decrees 'based on the principle of the separation of the Church from the State and the school from the Church';

(4) assistance to religious associations in resolving questions necessitating negotiations with such bodies as ministries.[18]

In addition, the Councils 'register the communities, arrange for the official transfer of prayer houses to existing, as well as to newly-organised, religious communities'.[19]

The resumption of organised theological instruction was permitted. At the end of 1943 the Orthodox Synod proposed to open a Theological Institute in Moscow with a three-year course to train future bishops and other religious leaders, as well as two-year courses in the dioceses.[20] On June 14, 1944, the Theological Institute was opened at the same time as a Theological Course in the Novodevichi Monastery, which was to function as a seminary training volunteer candidates.[21]

In September, 1944, the rules on religious instruction of children were given a more liberal interpretation. Karpov stated:

'Parents may themselves give children religious instruction . . . or send them to the homes of priests for such education. Children of different families may also gather in groups to receive religious instruction.'[22]

When Patriarch Sergei died on May 15, 1944, Metropolitan Aleksei became *locum tenens*. A new *Sobor* met in Moscow in early February, 1945, attended by the three Russian Metropolitans, 41 bishops and archbishops and 126 representatives of the Orthodox clergy and laity, and several distinguished foreigners. Metropolitan Aleksei was unanimously elected Patriarch.[23]

The Soviet leaders used the occasion to parade their tolerance. State assistance was given to entertain the foreign guests and Karpov greeted the *Sobor* on behalf of the Government, praising the patriotic efforts of the Church and promising his Council's good offices for the future.[24] The *Sobor* issued an appeal, 'To the Peoples of the Whole World', which showed how the Church was expected to support the foreign political line of the Government. The participants in the *Sobor* 'raise their voices against the efforts of those, particularly the Vatican', who were said to be assisting the perpetuation after the war of anti-Christian Fascist doctrines.[25]

The war led to a revival of religion, and particularly of Orthodox Christianity, in the USSR. By June, 1945, according to Karpov, the number of Orthodox churches had risen to 16,000.[26] Whereas in Moscow there were only 20 churches functioning in the winter of 1941,[27] by Christmas, January, 1944, there were about 50.[28]

Because of the favour shown it by the Soviet State, the Orthodox Church greatly increased its international influence and prestige. In December, 1944, the Orthodox of the Carpatho-Ukraine, formerly under the jurisdiction of the Serbian Orthodox Church, asked to become part of the Russian Church.[29] Good relations with the Serbian Church itself were established at the *Sobor* of 1945. Special efforts were made in regard to the Bulgarian Orthodox Church whose Exarch, in September, 1944, blessed the new, anti-fascist Government that ousted the King, thanked the Russian people for liberating Bulgaria, and received Acting Patriarch Aleksei's blessing in return.[30]

In the Near East close ties with the Orthodox were established before and during the 1945 *Sobor*. In May, 1944, many Russian Orthodox monks and nuns in Jerusalem accepted the authority of the Moscow Patriarch.[31]

[37]

(b) 1945–1953

The post-war policy of the Soviet leaders towards religion combined elements of both their wartime and pre-war attitudes. On the one hand, the Churches were permitted to retain, and even to improve, the position they had achieved during the war, at the price of public support for the domestic and foreign policies of the Kremlin; on the other hand, the campaign against religion was resumed.

There were favourable Government measures in the postwar years, too. A decree of August 15, 1945, granted the Churches the right to acquire objects needed for divine service and to build, rent or acquire Church buildings, local Soviets being required to assist in repairing and improving such buildings.[32] On February 22, 1946, the Government of the RSFSR decreed the ending of taxes on monastery buildings and lands.[33]

In these conditions the Orthodox Church at first continued to grow. By 1948 the number of its parishes had risen to 22,000 and of its monastic institutions to 89.[34] Orthodox theological education was considerably expanded. By 1946, in addition to theological academies in Moscow and Leningrad, there were four seminaries (Moscow, Leningrad, Odessa and Zhirovsti).[35] Four more were subsequently established.[36] On August 21, 1951, Metropolitan Nikolai told a delegation of British women that the Church had more than 20,000 churches, about 90 monasteries and nunneries, two academies and eight seminaries.[37] In 1946–1947 the Moscow Seminary had 124 students;[38] in 1950 it had a graduating class of 38.[39] The Leningrad Seminary began full-scale instruction in 1946 with 74 students and 13 instructors.[40]

As to the religious instruction of children, since it might not be given in schools or Church buildings, priests often gave private lessons.[41]

Church attendances remained high. Reports early in 1947 spoke of one Orthodox church filled with 'a sea of people and souls' and of another so crowded that 'one could not raise one's hand to make the sign of the Cross'. During Lent and Eastertide there was 'an unbelievable overfilling of the churches'. Some 400,000 faithful received Communion in the Orthodox cathedral in Leningrad at Easter.[42]

In enhancing its prestige and influence, the Orthodox Church continued to enjoy the backing of the Soviet Government. The authorities forcibly made an end of the Union of Brest, whereby in 1596 a large body of Orthodox clergy and laymen had accepted Papal authority while retaining their Orthodox rites and practices (*see* section on Catholicism). Abroad every effort was made to assert the leadership of the Russian Patriarch over the sister Orthodox Churches of the Balkans and the Near East. To this end Patriarch Aleksei and Metropolitan Nikolai were given facilities to make and receive several foreign visits. In May, 1945, 'with the assistance of the Soviet Government',[43] these hierarchs visited the Patriarchs of Antioch, Jerusalem, Alexandria and Damascus.[44] In June, the Bulgarian Exarch visited Moscow,[45] followed by the Rumanian Patriarch a year later.[46] In 1946 Patriarch Aleksei flew to Bulgaria for a 10-day visit.[47]

Complete submission to the Soviet régime was the price the Church had to pay for its toleration. On the 800th anniversary of Moscow, in 1947, the Patriarch sent to 'highly esteemed Joseph Vissarionovich, the Great Chief of our State', the Church's 'warmest wishes for health, for unvarying success in Your great work for the good of the Motherland, for the happiness of its peoples'.[48]

On Stalin's 70th birthday in 1949 prayers for Stalin were said in all Orthodox churches and he was presented with an 'Address of Greeting from the Clergy and Laymen of the Russian Orthodox Church'.[49]

In 1947 the Church openly took sides in the international arena:

'The international scene is growing clearer, the outlines of two camps, of labour and capital, are plainly visible. . . . Is there any need to ask in which camp the Russian Orthodox Church will remain?. . . With all her inner truth, she is on the side of those for whom labour is a matter of honour and of heroism, on the side of the oppressed in their striving to free themselves from enslavement by capital.'[50]

It has since continued to align itself publicly with Soviet foreign policy objectives and has played an active part in approved 'peace' movements.

When, for example, North Korea attacked South Korea the Patriarch and the Synod protested to the United Nations' Security Council. Their message said the Russian Orthodox Church 'cannot but express its condolence to the suffering country, and protests against American aggression in Korea. . . . The Russian Orthodox Church decisively condemns this

[39]

interference and the resulting inhuman annihilation of the peaceful population of Korea by American aviation'.[51]

Such complete co-operation and loyalty brought the Churches toleration of their existence, but not toleration of religion as such. In 1947 it was authoritatively stated:

'The measures of the Soviet Government in relation to the life of the Church . . . do not violate the fundamental decree of the Soviet régime on the separation of the Church from the State and the school from the Church, nor do they signify in any degree whatsoever that the Communist Party and the Soviet State have changed their attitude to religion and religious prejudices, which are still fairly widespread among the population.'[52]

The campaign against religion had been resumed as early as September, 1944, when the Party Central Committee issued a directive 'On the Organisation of Scientific Educational Propaganda' in order to 'overcome the survivals of ignorance, superstition and prejudice'.[53] Propaganda was to be based on 'the materialist explanation of natural phenomena, elucidation of the achievements of science, technology and culture'.[54]

In 1945 the Central Committee again 'drew the attention of all Party, Soviet and public organisations to the need for broad development of scientific enlightening work among the masses, the arrangement of lectures on natural scientific themes, the ceaseless unmasking of superstitions and prejudices'.[55] In 1948 *Pravda* declared:

'The insufficiently aggressive character of scientific propaganda is manifested from time to time in the failure to emphasise the struggle against religious prejudices. . . . Freedom of conscience . . . certainly does not signify that our political and scientific organisations are neutral in their attitude towards religion.'[56]

This statement inaugurated an intensification of the anti-religious effort which coincided with the first signs of stagnation in the growth of the Orthodox Church. Denunciations of religion in the Press and over the radio became open and bitter. Action was taken against Communists participating in religious ceremonies. In 1948, for instance, 49 people, among them some with secondary and higher education, were expelled from the Georgian Communist Party 'for the observance of religious rites'.[57]

At the same time it became clear that the Party leaders had confused their followers by their opportunistic *rapprochement* with the Churches, particularly the Orthodox Church. Steps were taken to dispel this confusion:

'It is sometimes asked whether the assertion that religion is harmful is not out of date; for the Church takes up an entirely loyal position in relation to the Soviet system, and the most prominent members of the Orthodox Church are among the partisans of peace.... Nevertheless religion remains religion. Even in our Socialist conditions religious morality continues to play a reactionary role. It clings to everything old, outworn and dead.... Religion hampers victory over all other survivals of the past. The Communist education of the workers is, therefore, inseparably linked with the exposure of religious morality.'[58]

Closely allied with the Soviet school in the atheistic indoctrination of children was the Komsomol. It was now explicitly stated: 'A young man cannot be a member of the Komsomol unless he is free of religious convictions.... For a member of the Komsomol it is impossible and inadmissible to believe in God and to observe religious rites.'[59] Leaders of Komsomol study circles were instructed: 'Komsomol members must be not only atheists and opponents of all superstition, but must actively combat the spread of superstitions and prejudices among youth.'[60]

In March, 1949, N. A. Mikhailov, then Secretary of the Komsomol Central Committee, reported to the 11th Komsomol Congress that there were signs of 'increased activity on the part of churchmen' to strengthen their influence over youth. Certain Komsomol organisations were 'impermissibly' ignoring this. They must 'greatly improve' scientific propaganda work.[61] The congress resolved 'to intensify the propaganda of natural science among youth and to conduct a persistent daily struggle against religious prejudices'.[62]

At the 19th Party Congress in October, 1952, Mikhailov, noting that 'attempts have been made to bring alien influences to bear on young people', stated: 'Young boys and girls have come under the influence of religion.' He promised that the Komsomol would 'improve ideological work among the masses of young people' in order to educate them 'in the spirit of Communism'.[63]

'Considerable work in the struggle against religious survivals' was also carried on by the All-Union Society for the Dissemination of Political and Scientific Knowledge set up in May, 1947.[64] Designed to involve the intelligentsia in the party's drive to indoctrinate the populace, one of the Society's functions was to develop to the full the 'right' of anti-religious propaganda guaranteed by the Constitution. Thus it was the direct, though unacknowledged, heir of the League of Militant Godless.

The interest of Agitprop in stepping up the Society's atheistic propaganda was made apparent. Its then Deputy Director, and former Secretary of the Militant Godless League, Oleshchuk, wrote in the Society's periodical:

'Particularly great in this respect are the tasks of the Society ... all the activities of which are directed to Communist education ... Propaganda for atheism is the task of all members of the Society. It must be conducted unflaggingly, systematically, on a broad front.'[65]

In August, 1950, it was reported that the Society was to launch a new, intensive drive against 'the medieval Christian outlook'. Propagandists would be sent to all the Republics with anti-religious films and 29,000,000 copies of pamphlets would be distributed.[66]

The trade unions, too, played their part, though not apparently on such a scale as before the war. As late as January, 1953, many of them were being accused of 'still underestimating the significance of questions of ideology', and were reminded that the 'whole activity' of their cultural institutions should be 'directed to the Communist education of the workers and to overcoming survivals of capitalism in people's consciousness'.[67]

The tenor of the first post-war anti-religious campaign was well conveyed by the publications of the Committee for the Affairs of Cultural-Enlightenment Establishments of the RSFSR. This governmental agency did much to supply atheist material for cultural institutions of all sorts. The Publishing House of Cultural-Enlightenment Literature put out a 'little library to assist the lecturer', a typical example of which was a pamphlet 'The Origin and Class Essence of Christianity', pre-scribing for lectures on this subject the following 'tasks':

'(1) Show that Jesus Christ, accepted by believers as the founder of Christianity, never existed in reality.

(2) Show that Christianity arose as the result of the long process of disintegration of the ancient slave-owning society, as a fantastic, distorted reflection of the apparent helplessness of the oppressed and exploited masses of the workers in the struggle against the oppressors and exploiters.

(3) Show that Christianity from the beginning of its existence always played a reactionary role, that the social principles of Christianity justified ancient slavery, acclaimed medieval serfdom, defended and defend today in bourgeois countries the hired slavery of capital; show that the Christian Church always took and takes today, especially in the person of the Vatican, an active part in all measures of the ruling exploiter classes directed to the oppression and enslavement of the workers.

(4) Show that in our country Christianity with its anti-scientific world-outlook and reactionary morality does great harm, like all other religious survivals, to the cause of the Communist education of the workers.'[68]

SOURCES

1. *Religious Communities in the Soviet Union*, p. 2.
2. *Pravda o Religii*, pp. 16–17.
3. *B.S.E.*, 1st edn., Vol. on the USSR, p. 1780.
4. *Pravda o Religii*, p. 84.
5. *Ibid.*, p. 168.
6. *New York Times*, January 5, 1943.
7. *Zhurnal Moskovskoi Patriarkhii* (hereafter cited as *Zh. M.P.*), 1944, No. 4, p. 5.
8. *B.S.E.*, 1st edn., Vol. on the USSR, p. 1780.
9. *Patriarkh Sergei*, p. 90.
10. *Ibid.*, p. 85.
11. *Ibid.*, p. 90.
12. *Pravda o Religii*, p. 216.
13. *Pravda*, November 4, 1942.
14. *Izvestiya*, September 5, 1943.
15. *Zh. M.P.*, 1943, No. 1, p. 6.
16. *Izvestiya*, October 8, 1943.
17. *Izvestiya*, July 1, 1944.
18. *B.S.E.*, 1st edn., Vol. on the USSR, p. 1788.
19. Spasov, p. 24.
20. *Zh. M.P.*, 1943, No. 3, pp. 22–24.
21. *Zh. M.P.*, 1944, No. 7, pp. 10–18.
22. *Christian Science Monitor*, September 30, 1944.
23. *Patriarkh Sergei*, pp. 322–331.
24. *Zh. M.P.*, 1945, No. 2, pp. 10–11; *Izvestiya*, February 4, 1945.
25. *Izvestiya*, February 10, 1945.
26. *New York Times*, June 7, 1945.
27. Curie, pp. 144–145.
28. *New York Times*, January 8, 1944.
29. *Zh. M.P.*, 1945, No. 1, pp. 5–10.
30. *Ibid.*, 1944, No. 10, pp. 6–7.
31. *New York Times*, May 9, 1944.
32. *Gurian*, pp. 156–157.
33. *New York Times*, February 24, 1946.

34. USSR *Information Bulletin*, Washington, January 28, 1949, pp. 54–56.
35. *Russky Golos*, December 1, 1946.
36. Spasov, p. 23.
37. *Soviet Monitor*, August 22, 1951.
38. *Zh. M.P.*, 1947, No. 7, pp. 35–38.
39. *Zh. M.P.*, 1950, No. 8, pp. 68–69.
40. *Zh. M.P.*, 1947, No. 7, pp. 44–46.
41. *Vestnik Russkogo Zapadno-Evropeiskogo Patriarshego Eksarkhata*, 1947, No. 2, pp. 15–20.
42. *Ibid.*
43. Spasov, p. 27.
44. *Zh. M.P.*, 1945, No. 8, pp. 6–25; No. 9, pp. 16–25.
45. *Zh. M.P.*, 1945, No. 9, pp. 29–44.
46. *New York Times*, October 22, 1946.
47. *Zh. M.P.*, 1946, No. 6, pp. 3–19.
48. *Zh. M.P.*, 1947, No. 10, p. 3.
49. *Ibid.*, pp. 11–13.
50. *Zh. M.P.*, 1947, No. 11, p. 33.
51. *Zh. M.P.*, 1950, No. 3, pp. 3–4.
52. *B.S.E.*, 1st edn., Vol. on the USSR, p. 1780.
53. *Propagandist*, 1944, No. 18, pp. 1–5.
54. Kolonitsky, pp. 30–31.
55. *B.S.E.*, 2nd edn., Vol. 2, p. 512.
56. *Pravda*, June 28, 1948.
57. *Zarya Vostoka*, January 28, 1949.
58. *Molodoi Bolshevik*, 1951, No. 21, p. 61.
59. *Komsomolskaya Pravda*, October 18, 1947.
60. *Komsomolsky Rabotnik*, 1947, No. 11, p. 27.
61. *Pravda*, March 30, 1949.
62. *Pravda*, April 16, 1949.
63. *Pravda*, October 7, 1952.
64. *B.S.E.*, 2nd edn., Vol. 2, p. 512.
65. *Nauka i Zhizn*, 1949, No. 11.
66. *Leningrad Radio*, August 27, 1950.
67. *Trud.*, January 27, 1953.
68. Amosov, p. 59.

III
Religion Since Stalin's Death

The relative tolerance for religion which had marked Stalin's last years did not long outlast his death. A Decree of the CPSU Central Committee 'On Major Shortcomings in Scientific Atheistic Propaganda and Measures for Improving it',[1] passed on July 7, 1954, denounced the neglected state of anti-religious work which had led to an 'increase in the number of citizens attending religious festivals and observing religious ceremonies'; its subsequent call for effective action gave rise to such an outburst of anti-religious excesses that the Party Central Committee had to issue a further decree only four months later.*

The decree of November 10, 1954, was headed 'On Mistakes in the Conduct of Scientific Atheistic Propaganda among the Population' and was signed personally by Khrushchev. Like the directives of 1923 (see p. 16), this Decree condemned the ridiculing of religious people and the use of administrative action in the anti-religious compaign, in the first place because such action was necessarily counter-productive, seeing that 'administrative measures and insulting attacks on believers and Church ministers ... can only lead to the consolidation and intensification of their religious prejudices.' It was, moreover, 'stupid and harmful to cast political doubt on particular Soviet citizens because of their religious convictions', now that a loyal Church had emerged in the Soviet Union. The Decree called for a marked improvement in the quality and effectiveness of anti-religious propaganda, without any relaxation in its intensity.[3]

* In June, 1955, Karpov, Chairman of the Council for the Affairs of the Russian Orthodox Church, admitted to a delegation of English churchmen that priests and citizens in various parts of the USSR had in the months following the earlier decree sent complaints to his office about cases of intereference and oppression.[2]

During the following two or three years this aim was pursued within the letter and spirit of the Decree. Personal attacks on ministers generally ceased and aberrations on the part of local atheists were condemned. In December, 1954, for example, the Director of the Central Lecture Bureau of the Latvian Ministry of Culture was criticised for including anecdotes about the clergy in his lectures. By so doing, he had insulted the feelings of believers and the clergy.[4] In February, 1957, a Komsomol secretary in Byelorussia condemned 'hooligan attacks on the clergy and believers while they were performing religious ceremonies', and deplored the fact that local Komsomol members had been responsible for a brass band playing marches and dance music outside the doors of a Catholic church on the Khrushchev collective farm in the Berestovitsa district during a service. He also re-emphasised the point that 'criticism of the improper behaviour of a priest in daily life . . . is not a criticism of religion and improper stories about religion can only annoy believers'.[5]

In this period, too, increasing use was made of statements by religious leaders in support of Soviet foreign policy, and a number of minor concessions were made to religious organisations. In January, 1956, the first new edition of the Orthodox Prayer Book to be published since the Revolution was on sale in Leningrad, and in the following May the Orthodox Church was allowed to publish a new edition of the Bible, the first since 1918, and also a combined New Testament and Psalter.

Concurrently, measures were taken to increase the effectiveness and volume of anti-religious propaganda. In 1955 the Society for the Dissemination of Political and Scientific Knowledge organised some 120,000 atheistic lectures.[6] Soviet publishing houses produced 187 books and pamphlets on scientific-atheistic themes with a circulation running into millions of copies.[7] Greater use was also made of the Museum of the History of Religion and Atheism in the former Kazan Cathedral in Leningrad. In the years 1955–56 this museum expanded substantially with the addition of sections on 'Soviet Natural Science against Religion', 'Religion and Atheism in Ancient Greece and Rome', 'The Origin of Christianity', 'The Origin of Religion', 'The Religions of China, India and Japan', 'The Religions of the Peoples of Tsarist Russia (Islam, Judaism etc.)'

[46]

and 'The Overcoming of Religious Survivals in the USSR'. The number of visitors conducted round it was radically stepped up. In 1954–56 the museum had 1,000,000 visitors as compared with the pre-war yearly average of 70,000.[8]

While these measures succeeded for a time in increasing the output of anti-religious propaganda, they did little to compensate for the general lack of militancy which followed the November, 1954, Decree and gradually there was a general falling off in the volume of propaganda. The number of atheistic lectures given by the Society for the Dissemination of Political and Scientific Knowledge dropped to 84,000 in 1956, and the number of anti-religious books and pamphlets published fell to 145 in 1956 and 102 in 1957. In 1957, only 31 atheistic books were published by 13 of the 15 Soviet republics.[9]

In May, 1957, the failure of the campaign to make any notable impact was officially acknowledged at an All-Union Conference and Seminar in Moscow on the tasks of anti-religious propaganda. M. B. Mitin, a leading Soviet ideologist and Chairman of the All-Union Society for the Dissemination of Political and Scientific Knowledge, declared that:

'In spite of the decisions of the Central Committee of the Soviet Communist Party on the intensification of atheistic propaganda, the number of lectures on atheism and their relative proportion in the subject matter of the Society has been considerably reduced. Some of the directors of local branches and some of the lecturers have not grasped the sense of the decisions of the Central Committee of November 10, 1954, and have slackened the struggle against religious survivals, presumably assuming that it is impossible to conduct a struggle against religion without conducting a struggle against the clergy ... The broad expansion of anti-religious propaganda is also hampered by the mistaken view held by a certain section of lecturers that religion will die out of its own accord ... Religion is not dying out of its own accord. On the contrary, there is a partial revival of religion as a result of the relaxation of our struggle against it.'[10]

NEW ONSLAUGHT ON RELIGION

Shortly afterwards this lull in the anti-religious campaign ended. From the late 1950s to 1964 the campaign was progressively intensified and the methods of persuasion and pressure used often paid little regard to the injunctions in the November, 1954, Decree. The strictures levelled against Stalin for his

[47]

'softness' towards religion, and, on the practical side, the revocation of tax and other concessions made to religious organisations 'in 1943–44 and the following decade' as being 'deviations from Leninist legislation' were tokens of this increased militancy.[11] Shortly after Khrushchev's fall in 1964, however, it had to be admitted once again that crude administrative methods had proved self-defeating.[12]

Anti-religious propaganda, although less strident after 1964, has continued unabated. During the last decade its volume has increased markedly. In the first nine months of 1959 the Society for the Dissemination of Political and Scientific Knowledge (since June, 1963, restyled the 'Znanie' or 'Knowledge' Society) gave 335,000 atheistic lectures, *i.e.*, four times the number it sponsored throughout 1956.[13] In 1963 the Society organised about 660,000 atheistic lectures.[14] Similarly the number of atheistic books published rose from 102 in 1957 to 264 in 1958 and to 336 in 1962, when their total circulation was 5,845,000 copies. In 1964, however, the number dropped to 285 with a circulation of 4,438,000.[15]

A wide variety of specialised bodies has been established to improve the theoretical level of atheistic propaganda and the training of propagandists. In 1963 Moscow housed among others:

(a) the Sector of the History of Religion and Atheism of the USSR Academy of Sciences' Institute of History;
(b) the Anti-Religious Sector of the Institute of Philosophy;
(c) the Scientific Atheistic Section attached to the Board of the All-Union 'Znanie' Society;
(d) the Scientific Atheistic Section at the Moscow Planetarium;
(e) the Scientific Atheistic Editorial Board of the State Publishing House of Political Literature;
(f) the offices of the journal *Nauka i Religiya*; (*see below*);
(g) the Department of Scientific Atheism in the Faculty of Philosophy at Moscow State University;
(h) the Anti-Religious Faculty of Moscow's University of Marxism-Leninism;
(j) a House of Scientific Atheism. (This was established late in 1963 as 'a real school for anti-religious propagandists.')[16]

In mid-1964 an Institute of Scientific Atheism of the Academy of Social Sciences attached to the CPSU Central Committee was set up to direct and co-ordinate work in this sphere. This was described as 'an important Party measure to improve atheist propaganda'.[17]

The 'Znanie' Society has, since September, 1959, been purveying material and advice to propagandists through its special atheist monthly *Nauka i Religiya* (Science and Religion), the circulation of which had risen by July, 1966, to 230,000, as compared with its original 70,000.

A network of new organisations has also been established to act as focal points for anti-religious work. This process began in September, 1957, with the opening of a House of the Atheist in Odessa. Since then Houses of the Atheist, Atheist Clubs and Universities of Atheism have proliferated. The militancy these institutions are designed to promote can be gauged from the Statutes of the Atheists Club in Danilov, a town in the Yaroslavl Region to the north of Moscow. These stipulate that every member must (*a*) personally take part in carrying out anti-religious propaganda; (*b*) be implacable towards all manifestations of religious prejudices at his work and in everyday life, struggle against the performance of religious ceremonies and religious festivals and dissuade people from going to church; (*c*) constantly broaden his outlook in the field of scientific atheism.[18]

Anti-religious propaganda has placed special emphasis on Soviet scientific achievements as demonstrating the irreconcilability of science and religion. In the first issue of *Nauka i Religiya*, the Vice-President of the International Astronomical Union, Kukarkin, rejected the existence of the 'firmament of Heaven' on the grounds that the Soviet moon rocket had made no contact with it.[19] Two years later Khrushchev associated himself with this line of reasoning when he declared in an interview:

'As for paradise in heaven, we had heard a lot about it from the priests. So we decided to find out for ourselves what it was like there, and we sent up our pioneer, Yury Gagarin. He circled the globe and found nothing in outer space. "It's pitch dark there", he said. "No garden, nothing like paradise." So we decided to send up another pioneer. We sent German Titov and told him to fly for a whole day. After all, Gagarin was up there for only an hour and a half and he might have missed paradise. "So you take a good look", we said. Well, he took off, came back and confirmed Gagarin's conclusion and reported that there was nothing there.'[20]

In November, 1963, Titov acknowledged at a meeting of the Party Central Committee's Ideological Commission that the repeated statements by cosmonauts that they had seen no God in the cosmos might carry little weight with the more sophisticated.[21] Nevertheless, in April, 1964, Gagarin, who had previously given his name to an atheists' club in Moscow, described how he had received 'a stream of letters' from former believers telling how Soviet exploits in space had led them to renounce their faith.[22]

To give the atheistic message greater appeal formal lectures have been supplemented with visits to planetariums, evenings of questions and answers and television quizzes. The resumption of the practice common in the 1920s of holding open debates with ministers of religion has, however, been discouraged on the grounds that 'Our Houses of Culture should not be turned into temples nor the lecturers' chair into a pulpit'.[23] Similarly the usefulness of the revival in many places of 'literary courts' has been questioned. These 'courts', which originated in the 1930s, stage simulated public trials of fictional religious characters in an anti-religious book. One such 'trial', in Chelyabinsk in 1963, which had ended in passionate calls for the defendants to be shot, drew the complaint that it brought atheistic propaganda down to the level of pure farce.[24]

Use has also been made of entertainment media, particularly of the cinema. One innovation has been the production of anti-religious 'documentaries'. Of these *The Road from Darkness*, produced by the Alma-Ata film studio and given a wide showing in 1961, began by showing Archimandrite Afanasy and Father Dmitry conducting a service at the local Cathedral of St. Nicholas and then in the empty church dividing up the receipts 'which enables them to lead a comfortable and far from ascetic life'.[25] In all 70 atheistic films were on circuit in 1963.[26] Outside the cinema atheistic productions have ranged from the musical comedy *A Hundred Devils and a Girl*, written by T. D. Khrennikov, First Secretary of the Union of Soviet Composers,[27] to *The Divine Comedy*, an atheistic puppet play staged under the direction of the leading Soviet puppeteer S. V. Obraztsov.[28]

Repeated calls have been made to strengthen anti-religious education in the face of much local apathy. In November, 1963, Ilichev, Chairman of the Party Central Committee's Ideological

Commission,* declared that 'the atheist education of children' was still 'the weakest point in our work'.[29] The Commission was told that atheistic indoctrination of the young was often frustrated by teachers who were content to give a non-religious, rather than an anti-religious, education. It was also handicapped by the poor grounding many teachers had had in atheism.

The failings reported to the Ideological Commission were attributed in part to the unsatisfactory progress made in introducing courses in atheism in higher educational establishments since 1958.[30] On the recommendation of the Commission, the Party Central Committee approved the introduction of a compulsory course in the 'Bases of Scientific Atheism' in universities and higher medical, agricultural and pedagogical institutions from the beginning of the 1964–5 academic year.[31] Also a number of students in the history and philosophy faculties of all universities and teachers' training institutions would specialise in 'scientific atheism'.[32]

The standard course in the 'Bases of Scientific Atheism' laid down by the Ministry of Higher and Secondary Education was later considered inadequate for training teachers, who continued to be criticised for neglecting their atheist duties and reminded that the future atheist 'must be formed in school'.[33] Relapses into a non-religious approach to education, *Nauka i Religiya* said in 1966, went a long way to explain the 'alarming cases', albeit rare, of school-leavers 'seeking their future in spiritual seminaries'. Atheistic education must be pursued continuously 'from the first class to the last'.[34]

The Commission's call for increased "control in guarding children and adolescents from the influence of churchmen and from being forced by their parents to observe religious ceremonies' invited further direct interference in the family lives of religious people.[35] In February, 1964, a party journal in Kazakhstan gave an idea of the extent to which pressure was already used to prevent the young going to church in some localities:

'The Komsomols at the Ust-Kamenogorsk Pedagogical Institute have decided to ascertain which of the children go to church. To do this, they stroll around outside the church during religious feast-

* Since Khrushchev's removal this Commission appears to have been abolished.

days. When they see any parents bringing a child to church, they politely advise them to send him back home. As a rule the parents agree to this. But it does happen at times that a mother, or, more frequently, a grandmother, proves obstinate. In that case the Komsomols find out where the schoolboy or schoolgirl lives and which school he or she is at and they report it to the school, and there the teachers set about enlightening the parents.

On one of these strolls the Komsomols made the acquaintance of Tanya X, a seventh-former, whom her grandmother was forcibly dragging along to church. They might not have noticed Tanya who, wrapped up in a shawl, looked just like an old woman. But when the Komsomols heard "Grandmother, do I have to go there?" they immediately went up to find out what it was all about. It was already late and her grandmother could not take Tanya back home herself as she was afraid of being late for the Easter service. The Komsomols offered to take her home ... The Komsomols reported this case to the school and her teachers helped Tanya to rid herself of her grandmother's religious influence.'[36]

This type of action fully accorded with the statement by S. P. Pavlov at the 1962 Komsomol Congress that the constitutional right of freedom of conscience applied only to adults as 'no one can be allowed to maim a child spiritually'.[37] Cases have also been reported of children being 'isolated' from the harmful influence of believing parents and placed in boarding schools.[38]

A particular feature of the anti-religious campaign has been the direct onslaught on the membership of religious organisations through 'individual work with believers'. This takes the form of attempts by party officials or propagandists to secure the conversion of individual believers to atheism. For this 'the assignment of trained persons of authority for work in believer families'[39] has been recommended. A typical instance, cited in 1960, told how the Chairman of the local branch of the 'Znanie' Society in the village of Kozishcha had selected the newly demobilised son of the local priest as his target. After making friends with him and getting him to read atheistic literature, this official finally got him to publish a recantation of his faith in the local paper and had thereafter helped him to find work in another locality.[40] Not that this method is always successful. In December, 1963, the Trade Union Committee at the Proletarsky Works in Leningrad was criticised for failing to secure the recantation of one of its members, who had been expelled as soon as her religious views had become known and had been ' "worked on" at several meetings'.[41] Similarly, atheists in a

Rakhov cardboard factory were admonished in January, 1966, for the hastiness with which they abandoned individual persuasion for 'more effective methods' by which they succeeded in driving believers out of the factory.[42]

The call for 'individual work' is an open invitation for deliberate intrusions into the privacy of peoples' homes, although the latter is formally guaranteed under Article 128 of the USSR Constitution. Students taking university courses in Scientific Atheism undertake individual work as part of their practical training. In Kazakhstan, for example, they visit believers' homes 'in the capacity of book distributors'.[43] Doctors, who necessarily have access to large numbers of people in their homes, are frequently urged to combine such work with their professional duties.[44] In maternity homes and clinics, too, it is incumbent upon medical workers to warn mothers of the harm done to children's health by the christening ceremony.[45]

Attempts made as in the first years of Soviet rule to introduce secular ceremonies, to reduce the attraction of religious ceremonial, began again in 1957, and came into prominence late in 1959 with the establishment of the Leningrad 'Wedding Palace'. Since then a wide variety of civil ceremonies designed as counterparts to baptism, confirmation and religious marriages and funerals or to obscure religious feastdays, have been inaugurated by 'public commissions' attached to the executive committees of local Soviets. In the Zhitomir area in the Ukraine, for example:

'In order to intensify the anti-religious impact of the Festival of Spring, it is celebrated on the eve of and during Easter. A week of shock work and a campaign of planting trees and shrubs in public places are arranged to coincide with it, and at the same time propagandists and agitators hold talks and atheistic evenings and give lectures. And in the evenings, in the squares, parks and streets of the towns and villages, special Spring festivities are organised. Amateur dramatic groups perform and revolutionary and scientific atheistic films are shown.'[46]

In 1963, Leningrad was again the first to establish special 'Palaces of the Newly-born'. Here parents are presented with a special medal with a portrayal of Lenin in an armoured car backed by the River Neva on one side, and the baby's name and date of birth on the other. Provision is also made for the presentation of gifts from local trade union and Komsomol officials.[47]

The effectiveness of these measures has varied. The results of a survey carried out in the Vyborg district of Leningrad in 1963 showed that in recent years up to 25 per cent of all babies born had been christened. In 1964, however, the number of religious christenings had dropped by more than 35 per cent compared with 1963.[*][48] In the Central Russian town of Shuya in 1965, ten per cent of the babies born were said to have been christened as compared with 70 per cent two years previously.[49] It has been claimed that since the establishment of the Wedding Palace the proportion of weddings in Leningrad had gone down from 25 per cent. to 0·24 per cent. by 1963. In the Ukrainian town of Drogobych, where 70–80 per cent. of family ceremonies used to take place in church, only 18 out of 571 couples were said to have married in church in 1962, and only six out of 391 in 1963. In the same town only 162 out of 1,018 newly-born babies had been christened in 1962 and only 90 out of 705 in 1963.[50] But it has been acknowledged that elsewhere in the Ukraine, in the Volynia and Lvov areas, up to half of all marriages and burial ceremonies took place in church in 1963 and that in some parts of the Nikolaev and Sumy regions the number of religious observances had actually shown an increase in 1962.[51] Similarly it has been acknowledged that in the town of Tula a third of all newly-born babies are christened and that a third of the people who die there are given religious funerals.[52]

The new secular rites have apparently failed to match the emotional and aesthetic appeal of their religious counterparts. A Lvov atheist, G. Kelt, writing in *Komsomolskaya Pravda* in August, 1965, said that the 'millennial experience' of religion and its 'methods of psychological influence on the masses' should not be ignored. A new ritual was needed to replace church liturgy. This would not be a 'new religion', 'simply intellectual-emotional celebrations—an apotheosis of the genius of man'.[53] In June, 1966, *Nauka i Religiya* called for fewer and better secular ceremonies. A writer to the same journal described the unpopularity of the civil ceremonies in his village. Because of the summary treatment and lack of ritual, 'fewer

* It must be noted that this was attributed to improved work by Party and communal organisations following the survey rather than to the introduction of the ceremonial registration of births. It was clear from the report that pressure had been brought to bear upon 'offenders' whom the investigation had brought to light.

[54]

and fewer young couples' were coming to register their marriages and 'they had ceased to bring new-born babies altogether'.[54]

Criticisms continue to appear in the Press from time to time of Party and *Komsomol* members who still observe religious rites, particularly the christening ceremony, and have ikons hanging in their homes.[55] Blame is usually attributed to the desire to appease fanatical grandparents and relations, who are sometimes said to have children christened in secret while the parents are away at work.[56] It is obvious, however, that their influence is greatly exaggerated, and this standard explanation is likely to prove even less satisfactory as the old generation of *babushki* decreases.

Concurrently with the institution of secular ceremonies, direct measures were taken in many localities against religious observances thought to be particularly harmful. In the Ulyanovsk Region, for example, 650 activists were recruited in 1959 to bar the way to pilgrims to 'Nikolai's Mount' and offer them transport back to the nearest railway station. To replace the pilgrimage, a 'Festival of Spring', incorporating a concert and sports meeting, was held. A House of Rest for the local collective farmers and a Pioneers' camp were later built on the site of the former holy wells.[57] In 1962 pilgrimages to the Blue Spring near the village of Kliny in the Mogilev region of the Ukraine were finally banned by a decision of a collective farm meeting, after the closure of the local church had failed to deter pilgrims.[58]

This intensified campaign against religion also had its darker sides. From 1957 onwards increasing use was made of apostates to discredit religious belief and personal attacks on ministers of religion were resumed. These attacks became particularly prominent in 1959. In February a former village priest denounced the 'immoral and corrupt' behaviour of priests in the Orthodox Archdiocese of Alma-Ata and charged the former Archbishop Aleksei with embezzling 200,000 roubles. He asserted that not one of his former colleagues had believed in God or had lived a blameless life.[59]

In July, 1959, an open letter was sent to Sergius, Bishop of Astrakhan and Stalingrad, by a former diocesan priest accusing him of appropriating hundreds of thousands of roubles for his personal enrichment and of having lived in sin with 'adopted daughters' and 'nieces' selected for him by a local monk. This letter, which also denounced Mikhail, Bishop of Smolensk and Dorogobuzh, for large-scale embezzlement, was given wide publicity. On July 3 it was published in the Ukrainian newspaper *Pravda Ukrainy*, on July 11 in the central newspaper *Sovetskaya Rossiya* and on July 13 it was broadcast by the Moscow Home Service.

Virulent attacks on ministers of all faiths became a regular feature of the anti-religious campaign, although their tendency to replace all other forms of anti-religious newspaper articles was at times deplored in the party Press.[60]

In April, 1960, during an attack on the Orthodox monastery at Zagorsk, the Troitse-Sergeev Lavra, it was stated that:

> 'In the cells of the individuals who "have abandoned all worldly things" there are drunken orgies and disgusting debauchery. The former novice F, who ran away from this plague spot, writes about the monks—"They drink and engage in debauchery in their cells and go on all night". We have accidentally come into possession of the correspondence between two of the monks. The letters cannot be printed because they are one mass of indecent expressions.'[61]

In 1963 a booklet, *The Truth About the Pskov-Pechora Monastery*, put out by the State Publishing House of Political Literature in Moscow in an edition of 200,000 copies, told a tale of fighting and debauchery among the monks and of the 'parasitical life' they led at the expense of ingenuous believers.[62]

The helplessness of ministers against these attacks was demonstrated in September, 1960, when it was revealed that Ermogen, the Archbishop of Tashkent and Central Asia, had written to the editors of the main party daily in Uzbekistan to protest at the falsity of the attack made on him on July 10 for 'feathering his nest' at the expense of believers and of indulging in high living.[63] Not only were his letters not published but they were made the pretext for a further attack on the Archbishop, who was retired to a monastery shortly afterwards.[64]

In the same year a complaint by a member of the Orthodox Church that these character assassinations violated the injunctions of the November, 1954, Decree against 'offending the feelings of believers' was rejected by the atheists' journal. Religious people, it stated, had no reason for complaint seeing that the Soviet Press also castigated workers who were rogues.[65]

For some years after 1960, wide publicity was given to trials of ministers in order to discredit religious organisations—a technique which inevitably casts doubt on the validity of the charges made. On July 8, 1960, for example, a few days after the Supreme Court of the Tatar ASSR had sentenced Archbishop Job of Kazan to three years' imprisonment for tax evasions, *Izvestiya* published an article accusing him of collaborating with the Nazis, large-scale embezzlement and general debauchery. Identical charges were made in greater detail in the July issue of *Nauka i Religiya*, which had been signed for the Press even earlier, on June 25.

A particularly glaring instance of this technique occurred on February 9, 1961, when, three days after a priest in the town of Kizlyar had been sentenced to six months' imprisonment on charges of drunkenness, hooliganism and misappropriation of funds, *Makhachkala Radio* broadcast recorded excerpts of the transcript of his trial. These, among other things, impugned the Archbishop of Stavropol and Baku, and were accompanied by a commentary on the harmful and anti-social influence of the clergy. Capital was also made out of the trial of the Archbishop of Irkutsk the following summer on a charge of receiving stolen vaseline.[66]

In January, 1964, the trial of three priests in Orenburg charged with bribing officials for the purposes of tax evasion was again used to advertise the alleged debauchery and cynicism of priests in the diocese, one of whom was said to have openly drunk beer during a service in the cathedral. The trial itself, during which one of the defendant priests implored his wife from the witness box to incriminate him, had manifestly dubious overtones.[67]

Another feature reminiscent of earlier militant periods was the closure of churches and church institutions. In October, 1960, it was reported from the Ukraine that 17 churches had been closed in the Zaporozhe region following individual work with believers;[68] the following June it was stated that 100 churches and prayer-houses had been closed in the Dnepropetrovsk region 'at the request of the population' during the previous two years;[69] and in February, 1962, the claim was made that in the last few years 180 churches had been closed in the Volynia region in the Ukraine.[70] Other reports of Church closures came from Moldavia, where in December, 1960, it was stated that 18 out of 25 churches had been closed in one area[71] and in June, 1963, the Moldavian First Party Secretary claimed that 'the majority of churches have been closed' and that 'the inhabitants of twenty-three monasteries have left their cells'.[72] It has been estimated that half the Orthodox monasteries have been closed down in recent years.[73]* Between 1959 and 1964 the number of Orthodox seminaries was reduced from eight to four, and the exclusion of the Lutsk seminary from a list of seminaries given for the new academic year in the *Journal of the Moscow Patriarchate* in April, 1965, and May, 1966, substantiated reports that this seminary, too, has been closed. Admission requirements were listed only for the academies at Zagorsk (near Moscow) and Leningrad and the seminaries at Zagorsk, Leningrad and Odessa.[74]

In December, 1962, a document was published in West European newspapers purporting to be the text of an appeal by monks in the monastery of Pochaev against the persecution by Party officials.[75] It is known that physical methods of pressure have been used in the case of many of the thousands of churches closed in recent years. In December, 1961, the following account was given of the measures leading to the closing of a church in Magnitogorsk:

'Certain ministers in the town of Magnitogorsk seriously compromised themselves through immoral behaviour. News of this appeared in the local Press. The scientific-atheistic section of the town's branch of the society organised a series of lectures at the shops of the metallurgical combine, at the administration of the "Magnitostroi" Trust, at various enterprises and institutions and at workers' hostels. Evenings of questions and answers were held in the town's clubs. Widespread propaganda of scientific-atheistic knowledge and the explaining of difficult questions to believers and waverers led at first to the rejection of religion by many believers and finally also to the closing of one of the two churches in the town.'[76]

Further evidence of this kind of direct action is provided by the criticisms levelled against administrative measures when they misfire. In September, 1963, for example, *Nauka i Religiya* denounced the Executive Committee of the Soviet in Krasnograd, a town which had a strong Orthodox community. In February, 1962, the Committee had decreed that their prayer house and its lodge should be demolished on the pretext that the land was needed for new urban development. The be-

* The total figure of monasteries administered by all churches and faiths was given as 63 by a Moscow broadcast to S.E. Asia on March 27, 1964.

lievers were moved out but no reconstruction took place. The effect had been similar to an attempt 'to put out a fire with petrol'. The believers became still more 'fanatical' and eventually the Council for the Affairs of the Russian Orthodox Church attached to the USSR Council of Ministers had had to intervene to restore the prayer house to Krasnograd's Orthodox community, which was now stronger and more active than it had been before.

The action taken by the Executive Committee of the local Soviet in the Ukrainian town of Novomoskovsk was similarly condemned. On November 19, 1960, it had passed a resolution on the confiscation of the Church of the Trinity and its conversion into a museum of local history. Following this a further resolution had been passed rescinding the registration of the town's Orthodox community on the grounds that 'it had ceased its activities'. In fact, not only had the believers not left Novomoskovsk but their sense of injustice had increased their religious fervour. As for the town Soviet, it had lacked the means to establish a museum of local history and had quite recently turned this church, which was a fine piece of medieval architecture, into a school gymnasium!

But the most spectacular example cited emanated from Bashkiria:

'The atheists in the town of Davlekanov in the Bashkir ASSR have also cut the road between them and believers. In August, 1960, the local District Soviet Executive Committee passed a decision on the building of a cinema in the town on the exact site where the prayer house was situated. The believers were not even informed that their prayer house was to be demolished. Preparations for the confiscation of the temple were carried on in the deepest secrecy. And then on one fine day a group of activists arrived at the place, summoned the chairman of the [prayer-house's] executive organ, Alekseev, and handing him a document on the confiscation of the prayer house, hurriedly began to carry out the furniture. In his report at a Republican methodological conference, Comrade Kharchikov, one of the leaders of anti-religious work in the town, described this "operation" as follows: "They (*i.e.*, the believers) considerably obstructed the closing [of their prayer house] and while it was true that we succeeded in taking away the furniture more or less peacefully, the last lorry got away after certain difficulties. The believer activists, more than sixty of them, began to shower the District Soviet's Executive Committee with demands that their church should be opened and what scurrilities didn't they voice!"

[59]

It remains only to add that the prayer house building has now, more than three years later, still not been demolished. In it there has been organised a gymnasium for a nearby secondary school.

It is difficult now for even the most experienced propagandists of atheism to conduct individual work with believers.'[77]

In many localities congregations were not slow to take up the challenge. In July, 1963, the story was told of how a cross had appeared near a well in the Syasstroi industrial settlement near Leningrad. The local Soviet had ordered it to be removed and the well to be filled in. However, the next night unknown people had erected another and stouter cross in its place. This too was removed. Finally the 'sanctimonious people' had put up another cross made of steel from nails and on this occasion 'technical equipment' had had to be used to remove it. In the same area a House of Culture, about 300 metres from the local Church, had had to close its atheists' club because no one went there—and this is a short time after A. A. Osipov,* the most prominent apostate in the USSR, had visited it.[78]

Against the intensified onslaught, however, the religious organisations had little means of defence. The few religious periodicals, e.g., the *Journal of the Moscow Patriarchate*, omit all mention of the anti-religious campaign, for to do so would be to engage in 'religious propaganda' which is prohibited.

One counter-measure taken by religious leaders—the ex-communication by the Orthodox Church in December, 1959, of apostates and laymen who had committed blasphemy in public—was little more than a gesture,[79] though it may not have been coincidental that Karpov was replaced as Chairman of the Soviet Government's Council for the Affairs of the Russian Orthodox Church in the same month as the ordinance was published. (His successor, V. A. Kuroedov, was formerly First Party Secretary in the Sverdlovsk region and an authority on ideological work.)

* A. A. Osipov, formerly a Professor in Old Testament Studies at the Leningrad Theological Academy, publicly renounced his faith in *Pravda* in December, 1959. He subsequently appeared on radio and television and had many books, brochures and newspaper articles published. In December, 1963, however, he was criticised in *Nauka i Religiya* as having gone too far in describing God as 'a rascal, an insatiable brigand chief and a loathsome being' and all ministers without distinction as 'parasites, tricksters and chameleons' in his book, *The Catechism without Embellishment*.

This general impotence was further demonstrated in July, 1961, when, three months after the USSR Council of Ministers had directed the Patriarch's attention 'to the numerous cases of the violation by the priesthood of Soviet legislation on cults and pointed to the necessity of bringing appropriate order into the life of parishes', new parish regulations were approved at a special *Sobor* of Bishops,[80] the first to be called since 1945.

These regulations barred the local priest from participating in the financial administration of the parish and so manifestly lowered his authority, as three bishops pointed out.[81] By entrusting financial measures exclusively to the parish executive committees the regulations also opened the way for further pressure, as the authorities have always found it much easier to bring influence to bear on the lay leadership of the various religious organisations. As *Nauka i Religiya* put it:

'Of course it is easier to exert influence on the rank and file believer—he is as a rule "at our side", he works at our institution and at our enterprise. He can be worked on at a meeting and threatened with dismissal from his job. The religious professionals are another thing . . . They cannot be summoned to a trade union meeting. They cannot be threatened with dismissal.'[82]

DEVELOPMENTS SINCE KHRUSHCHEV'S FALL

Since Khrushchev's downfall there has been a critical reappraisal of anti-religious work. In 1965, a postmortem on the campaign's failings was begun in the pages of *Nauka i Religiya*, and crude discriminatory practices against believers were widely condemned. 'Understand in order to help'[83] became the order of the day and atheist workers were reminded that the majority of believers were 'honest workers, building Communism together with all Soviet people'.[84] 'There are millions of believers in our country,' *Nauka i Religiya* stated in June, 'but religious fanatics, who really deserve isolation from society, are very few.'[85]

Nevertheless, in the face of growing apathy among atheist workers, the kid-glove treatment of believers cannot be allowed to go too far. In May, 1966, for example, *Krokodil* rebuked Orel atheists for their failure to condemn the Deputy Director of the Orel *Oblast* Drama Theatre, who had been a Party member for more than twenty years and was also a believer.[86]

The bankruptcy of coercive measures such as the closure of

churches has been openly acknowledged. A remarkably frank *Komsomolskaya Pravda* article in August, 1965, stated:

'Today we are again lulling ourselves [by the thought that] many believers in our country have left the Church and religion. This is self-deception. It is true that in the great part of the Soviet Union's territory there are no churches and no servants of the cult. But believers there are. . . . The closing of a parish does not make atheists out of believers. On the contrary, it attracts people to religion all the more and furthermore embitters their hearts.'[87]

The same writer considered that believers were not impressed by renegade priests and that cases of genuine apostasy were 'very rare'.

In fact articles by apostates have become much less common in the Press and personal articles on Orthodox priests have practically disappeared. But while the Orthodox Church is hardly ever attacked by name, there is evidence that administrative pressure has continued. The text of open letters, said to have been sent by two Moscow priests to Patriarch Aleksei and President Podgorny at the end of 1965, was subsequently published in the West. In them the priests listed instances of persecution of the Orthodox Church which had contravened Soviet legislation and criticised the Church officials for their lack of effective resistance to the illegal activities of the Government's Council for the Affairs of the Russian Orthodox Church.[88] Later in 1966, the text of an encyclical addressed to 52 diocesan bishops was also made public. In it, the Patriarch deplored the actions of the priests, who were suspended from office in May.[89]

These letters confirmed reports of considerable opposition within the Orthodox Church to the policies of the official Patriarchy.[90] One dissident group which was already known to exist is the underground church of 'True Orthodox Christian Wanderers', a serial about which was carried by *Nauka i Religiya* in the first six months of 1966.

Despite the post-Khrushchev régime's apparent reluctance to intervene directly in religious matters by issuing central directives, there has nevertheless been some tightening up of administrative controls over religious communities. In March, 1966, the Presidium of the RSFSR Supreme Soviet announced two decrees and one resolution defining and supplementing existing legislation on religious cults. In effect, the first decree was little more than a clarification of certain offences against

the 1929 law 'Concerning Religious Associations'.* According
to the second decree, supplementing article 142 of the RSFSR
Criminal Code on the infringement of the law on the separation of Church from State and School from Church, anyone
guilty of a second or subsequent offence against this section or
of 'organisational activity aimed at committing such deeds' was
henceforward liable to a sentence of up to three years' deprivation of liberty.[91]

The resolution specified as offences against this law such
practices as compulsorily extracting dues for the benefit of
religious organisations or ministers, circulating literature calling for the non-fulfilment of Soviet legislation on cults, and
organising religious meetings, processions and other ceremonies
which violated public order. Another offence was vaguely defined as 'carrying out deceitful actions with the object of arous-
ing religious superstitions among the population'. In addition,
it was said to be an offence to discriminate against people, because of their religious beliefs, in matters such as employment
and the payment of bonuses. Instances of such abuse were
openly admitted by *Nauka i Religiya* in the first half of 1966.[92]

Similar decrees were subsequently published in other republics.[93] It is likely, however, that the new decrees were directed
not so much against the Orthodox Church as against more
militant sectarians, particularly the Baptists. (See section on
'Protestantism'.)

In December, 1965, the two religious Councils attached to
the USSR Council of Ministers—for the affairs of the Russian
Orthodox Church and of Religious Cults—were amalgamated
into a single body to be known as the Council for the Affairs
of Religion.[94] Writing in *Izvestiya* in August, 1966, Kuroyedov,
the Council's Chairman, said that as a result of the amalgamation 'the rôle and responsibility of the Council in the control
over the observance of legislation on cults had been significantly
increased and corresponding rights granted to it'.[95]

The task, set at the 22nd Party Congress, of completely overcoming 'religious prejudices' is still said to determine 'the
present stage in the struggle against religion.'[96] (The question
of anti-religious work was not raised at the 23rd Congress in
March, 1966.) However, this target is unlikely to be achieved
on time, *i.e.*, 1980, 'in the course of the struggle for Communism'.[97] In 1961, when the Russian Orthodox Church joined the

* See p. 21.

World Council of Churches, it claimed that it had 20,000 places of worship and 30 million 'regular adult worshippers'.[98] Of the five other churches in the USSR which joined the WCC in 1962, the Armenian Gregorian Church cited a total membership of 4,500,000, of which 1,400,000 were living outside the Soviet Union. The Georgian Orthodox Church gave no membership figures but stated that it had 100 churches.[99] (Figures for the Baptists and the Lutherans in Estonia and Latvia are given in the section on 'Protestantism'.)

SOURCES

1. *Voprosy Ideologicheskoi Raboty,* pp. 61–65.
2. Stanley G. Evans, *The Russian Church Today,* p. 8.
3. *Pravda,* November 11, 1954.
4. *Sovetskaya Latviya,* December 19, 1954.
5. *Molodoi Kommunist,* 1957, No. 2, p. 28.
6. *Nauka i Religiya,* 1960, No. 1, p. 4.
7. *Kommunist,* 1958, No. 7, p. 126.
8. *Voprosy Istorii Religii i Ateisma,* No. 5, pp. 413, 423.
9. *Kommunist,* 1958, No. 7, p. 126.
10. *Voprosy Filosofii,* 1957, No. 5, p. 223.
11. *Kommunist,* 1964, No. 1, p. 29.
12. *Komsomolskaya Pravda,* August 15, 1965.
13. *Nauka i Religiya,* 1960, No. 1, p. 4.
14. *Nauka i Religiya,* 1964, No. 6, p. 3.
15. See issues of Pechat SSSP for those years.
16. *Izvestiya,* November 1, 1963.
17. *Voprosy Istorii CPSU,* 1965, No. 1, p. 18.
18. *Nauka i Religiya,* 1960, No. 5, pp. 75–76.
19. *Nauka i Religiya,* 1959, No. 1.
20. *Pravda,* September 10, 1961.
21. *Nauka i Religiya,* 1964, No. 1, p. 57.
22. *Nauka i Religiya,* 1964, No. 4, p. 11.
23. *Nauka i Religiya,* 1960, No. 2, p. 85.
24. *Nauka i Religiya,* 1963, No. 1, p. 72.
25. *Nauka i Religiya,* 1961, No. 5, p. 90.
26. *Nauka i Religiya,* 1964, No. 1, p. 42.
27. *Nauka i Religiya,* 1961, No. 11, p. 93.
28. *Nauka i Religiya,* 1961, No. 12, pp. 90–91.
29. *Kommunist,* 1964, No. 1, p. 37.
30. *Ibid.,* p. 46.
31. *Partiinaya Zhizn,* 1964, No. 2, p. 23.
32. *Pravda,* March 2, 1964.
33. *Izvestiya,* November 26, 1965.

34. *Nauka i Religiya*, 1966, No. 9, p. 75.
35. *Partiinaya Zhizn*, 1964, No. 2, p. 26.
36. *Partiinaya Zhizn Kazakhstana*, 1964, No. 2, pp. 44–45.
37. *Pravda*, April 17, 1962.
38. *Komsomolskaya Pravda*, May 29, 1965 and November 25, 1966. *Izvestiya*, July 23, 1965.
39. *Kommunist*, 1964, No. 1, p. 34.
40. *Nauka i Religiya*, 1960, No. 11, p. 87.
41. *Leningradskaya Pravda*, December 7, 1963.
42. *Nauka i Religiya*, 1966, No. 2, p. 3.
43. *Politcheskoe Samoobrazovanie*, 1965, No. 3, p. 83.
44. *Partiinaya Zhizn*, 1966, No. 11, p. 57.
45. *Politcheskoe Samoobrazovanie*, 1965, No. 8, p. 126.
46. *Kommunist Ukrainy*, 1963, No. 11, p. 40.
47. *Leningradskaya Pravda*, August 29, 1963.
48. *Voprosy Filosofii*, 1965, No. 3, p. 89.
49. *Kommunist*, 1965, No. 15, p. 64.
50. *Nauka i Religiya*, 1964, No. 1, pp. 37, 39.
51. *Kommunist Ukrainy*, 1963, No. 11, pp. 36, 43.
52. *Selskaya Zhizn*, June 5, 1963.
53. *Komsomolskaya Pravda*, August 15, 1965.
54. *Nauka i Religiya*, 1966, No. 6, pp. 52–53.
55. *Nauka i Religiya*, 1966, No. 9, p. 56. *Partiinaya Zhizn*, 1966, No. 11, p. 59.
56. *Voprosy Filosofii*, 1965, No. 3, p. 89. *Nauka i Religiya*, 1966, No. 8, p. 48.
57. *Nauka i Religiya*, 1959, No. 1.
58. *Nauka i Religiya*, 1962, No. 9, p. 56.
59. *Kazakhstanskaya Pravda*, February 20, 1959.
60. *Pravda*, January 8, 1961.
61. *Trud*, April 17, 1960.
62. *Sovetskaya Estoniya*, June 4, 1963.
63. *Pravda Vostoka*, September 3, 1960.
64. *Zh. M.P.*, 1960, No. 10, p. 4.
65. *Nauka i Religiya*, 1960, No. 2, pp. 13–14.
66. *Nauka i Religiya*, 1962, No. 8, p. 27.
67. *Literaturnaya Gazeta*, January 21, 1964.
68. *Pravda Ukrainy*, October 20, 1960.
69. *Kommunist Ukrainy*, 1961, No. 6, p. 39.
70. *Izvestiya*, February 3, 1962.
71. *Sovetskaya Moldaviya*, December 13, 1960.
72. *Izvestiya*, June 7, 1963.
73. *Church Times*, March 26, 1964.
74. *Zh. M.P.*, 1965, No. 4, p. 47. *Zh. M.P.*, 1966, No. 5, p. 26.
75. *Discussione*, December 23, 1962.
76. *Nauka i Religiya*, 1961, No. 12, p. 87.
77. *Nauka i Religiya*, 1963, No. 9, pp. 77–78.
78 *Leningradskaya Pravda*, July 21, 1963.

79. *Zh. M.P.*, 1960, No. 2, p. 27.
80. *Zh. M.P.*, 1961, No. 8, p. 6.
81. *Ibid.*
82. *Nauka i Religiya*, 1963, No. 9, p. 4.
83. *Nauka i Religiya*, 1965, No. 9, p. 2.
84. *Sovetskaya Rossiya*, September 23, 1965.
85. *Nauka i Religiya*, 1965, No. 6, p. 37.
86. *Krokodil*, 1966, No. 15, p. 10.
87. *Komsomolskaya Pravda*, August 15, 1965.
88. *The Catholic Herald*, August 19, 1966.
89. *The Times*, August 26, 1966.
   Church Times, June 24, 1966.
90. *Church Times*, August 19, 1966. [Official silence on the rift was broken in October, 1966, with an attack in *Nauka i Religiya* on a lay theologian who had written an open letter to the Patriarch accusing the Orthodox hierarchy of subservience to the State.]
91. *Vedomosti Verkhovnogo Soveta RSFSR*, 1966, No. 12, pp. 219–220.
92. *Nauka i Religiya*, 1966, No. 2, p. 2.
   Nauka i Religiya, 1966, No. 6, p. 7.
93. *Sovetskaya Kirgiziya*, May 17, 1966.
   Turkmenia Iskra, June 28, 1966.
   Pravda Ukrainy, June 30, 1966.
   Sovetskaya Byelorussiya, July 25, 1966.
   Kazakhstanskaya Pravda, July 28, 1966.
   Pravda Vostoka, August 27, 1966.
   Bakinsky Rabochi, September 13, 1966.
   Sovetskaya Latviya, September 10, 1966.
   Sovetskaya Estoniya, September 18, 1966.
94. *Izvestiya*, December 18, 1965.
95. *Izvestiya*, August 30, 1966.
96. *Nauka i Religiya*, 1966, No. 3, p. 3.
97. *Nauka i Religiya*, 1961, No. 11, p. 6.
98. *World Christian Handbook*, p. 221.
99. *Current Developments in the Eastern European Churches* (hereafter cited as *Current Developments*), August–September, 1962, p. 5.

IV

Non-Orthodox Religions

━━━━━━━━━━━━━━━━━━━━━━━━━

(a) ISLAM

Islam has the second largest following in the Soviet Union. On January 1, 1912, there were within the Russian Empire 16,266,073 Muslims, including 4,635,000 in European Russia, 7,955,000 in Central Asia, 3,335,000 in the Caucasus and 120,000 in Siberia. There were then 24,321 Muslim communities and 26,279 mosques.[1] Soviet sources today give the number of Muslims in the USSR as 30,000,000,[2] but this figure would seem to be a total figure for Muslims by nationality rather than a measure of active religious affiliation. There is no official over-all figure for the number of mosques. But the fact that in 1959 there were no more than 200 central mosques and 1,000 district mosques in Soviet Central Asia,[3] as compared with the 12,000 mosques which existed in the province of Turkestan[4]* before the establishment of Soviet rule, gives an indication of the decrease which has taken place in the number of Islamic institutions. Most Soviet Muslims are Sunni, though there is a considerable Shia minority in Transcaucasia.[5]

The Soviet Communist Party has consistently subordinated its basic hostility to Islam, as a form of religious belief, to the needs of its internal and external policies. In 1957 the leading Soviet ideologist, M. B. Mitin, testified to the difficulties that Soviet overtures to the Arab world were causing anti-Islamic lecturers in the USSR, when he emphasised at an All-Union Conference on Questions of Scientific-Atheistic Propaganda:

'In demonstrating the anti-scientific character of Islam, we must at the same time take into consideration the part it is playing under present-day conditions, when under its banner there are a number

---

*Soviet Central Asia was then made up of the province of Turkestan and the vassal States of Khiva and Bokhara. The figure quoted does not include the 3,000 mosques in Khiva or the large number in the Bokharan Emirate. (The city of Bokhara alone had 360 mosques.)

[67]

of movements of great progressive importance, in particular the fight of the Arab peoples, led by Egypt, for their independence. In the Eastern countries there are still a large number of people whose religious sentiments fuse with their national sentiments. At the same time . . . it is essential to keep in mind that the imperialists try to use Islam for their own purposes in order to stir up enmity between the peoples, in order to weaken their forces in the fight for independence . . . From this it follows that our lecturers must have great political insight, a profound grasp of the contemporary social processes, in order to carry on a proper fight against Islam.'[6]

1917–1920

The basic Marxist attitude to Islam has long been formulated by Engels, who said, 'The religious revolution of Mohammed was, like *every* religious movement, reactionary.'[7] At first, however, immediate tactical considerations prevailed among the Bolsheviks. On November 24, 1917, the Soviet Government appealed 'To All Toiling Muslims of Russia and the East'[8] whose 'mosques and prayer-houses have been destroyed, whose beliefs and customs have been trampled on by the Tsars and the oppressors of Russia'. It promised:

'Your beliefs and customs, your national and cultural institutions are declared henceforth free and inviolable. Organise your national life freely and without hindrance. This is your right. Know that your rights . . . are protected by the entire might of the revolution and its organs . . . Support this revolution and its Government!'

The legal position of Muslim religious organisations was regulated by the decree of January 23, 1918, on the separation of the Church from the State.[9] At the same time a special People's Commissariat for Muslim Affairs was set up under Stalin's Commissariat of Nationalities.[10] In contrast to the active hostility then displayed towards the Orthodox Church, direct attacks on Islamic institutions or communities were not encouraged. For Lenin recognised that 'such peoples as the Kirghiz, Uzbeks, Tadzhiks, Turkmens' were 'still under the influence of their mullahs' and must be handled with great care.[11]

Most Muslims were in fact hostile or at least suspicious of the Soviet régime, particularly the Islamic peoples of the Northern Caucasus, because of their fear, based on what Soviet sources claim were 'slanderous rumours', that the régime would destroy the rites, laws and traditions by which they lived.[12] In November, 1920, Stalin hastened to make reassuring promises to the peoples of Daghestan and the adjacent Mountain Republic:

'Daghestan must be governed in accordance with its specific features, its manner of life and customs. We are told that among the Daghestan peoples the *Shari'ah*° is of great importance. We have also been informed that the enemies of Soviet power are spreading rumours that it has banned the *Shari'ah*. I have been authorised by the Government of the Russian Soviet Federative Socialist Republic to state here that these rumours are false. The Government of Russia gives every people the full right to govern itself on the basis of its laws and customs. The Soviet Government considers that the *Shari'ah*, as common law, is as fully authorised as that of any other of the peoples inhabiting Russia. If the Daghestan people desire to preserve their laws and customs, they should be preserved.'[13]

'If it is shown that the *Shari'ah* is necessary, then let the *Shari'ah* remain. The Soviet Government has no thought of declaring war on the *Shari'ah*.'[14]

At the time many Muslims took these promises at their face value. They were also misled by decrees (Turkestan, January 10, 1921; Azerbaidzhan, July 21, 1922, etc.) establishing Friday, the Muslim day of public prayer, in place of Sunday as the day of rest in predominantly Muslim regions.[15]

1921–1928

With the end of the Civil War the need for tolerance passed. The Commissariat of Nationalities was reorganised and the Commissariat for Muslim Affairs disappeared.[16] In the spring of 1921 'the policy of the party and the Soviet State in relation to Islam ... found brilliant expression' in the activity of Sergei Kirov, party plenipotentiary in the Caucasus, whose speeches 'played a great rôle in unmasking the class essence of Islam and its code of laws—the *Shari'ah*'.[17] On April 21 he addressed the Constituent Congress of the Soviets of the Mountain Republic. He began reassuringly enough, but when one delegate demanded: 'If you give us the *Shari'ah* give it fully and completely', Kirov replied only obliquely: 'You know that we admit the *Shari'ah* in order to strengthen the power of the workers. How you make it so is a question which does not interest us in any way. It is your affair.'[18]

° The *Shari'ah* is the Muslim canon law, a collection of religious statutes containing the Koranic laws (with commentaries).

[69]

The Communists now employed a tactic they were using against the Orthodox Church. In Daghestan there were about 40,000 Muslim religious leaders and officials. To disrupt such an important group the party encouraged a 'progressive' pro-Soviet schism advocating revision of the *Shari'ah*. In 1923 the schismatics held a congress and sent a message of allegiance to Lenin:

'The Congress ... greets thee, leader of the great army of the toilers, liberating the whole world from the chains of slavery and disgrace. We believe in the victory of thine army. We believe that Islam will be freed from oppression with its help ... We shall help thine army.'[19]

These illusions were soon shattered when the Commissariat for the *Shari'ah* was abolished, the religious schools liquidated and, in 1925–1926, the registration of births, deaths and marriages transferred from the Muslim to the Soviet authorities. From the first, limitations had been placed on the *Shari'ah* courts; now these were 'finally liquidated' and 'the Soviet Government began a decisive struggle against the *Shari'ah*'.[20]

The first Soviet books on Islam began to appear, their purpose being to 'show the crimes perpetrated against the people by the Muslim priesthood on the orders of the enemies of the Soviet régime'.[21]

Many of these early works were already 'permeated with a militant spirit; they unmasked all sorts of religious fairy-tales about miracles, holy men and prophets, revealed the reactionary, counter-revolutionary face of the Muslim priesthood'.[22]

This activity was in line with the resolution of the 12th Party Congress (April, 1923) 'On the State of Anti-Religious Agitation and Propaganda':

'Taking into account that the 30-million Muslim population of the Union of Republics has preserved almost untouched to this day numerous mediaeval prejudices, linked with religion and used for counter-revolutionary purposes, it is essential to work out forms and methods of liquidating these prejudices, taking into account the peculiarities of the different nationalities.'[23]

Caution was the watchword of the party's campaign against Islam at this time. The 13th Congress (May, 1924) warned that 'a careful attitude is particularly necessary in the Eastern republics and regions'[24] because, as a modern Soviet commentator explains, in those areas 'Muslim traditions and religious survivals of all sorts still represented a serious force and the Muslim priesthood still enjoyed great authority and influence'.[25]

At the end of the 1920s 'the laws and traditions of Islam . . . continued to play a very great rôle in the private life of the people'.[26] Since they were incompatible with the policies embodied in the First Five-Year Plan semi-tolerance was now replaced by an all-out attack. This formed part of the general anti-religious campaign and the same methods were used. In 1929 it was reported from Azerbaidzhan that 'transfers of mosques for cultural purposes have occurred not only in places where public, cultural and educational work is well organised but also in the most backward villages, where the influence of the *mullahs* is still strong. Mosques in the Zakataly *uyezd* (district), the Khillia sub-division of the Salyan *uyezd* (15 in the latter) and the Geokchai *uyezd*, the huge Dzhume mosques in Salyamy, and the mosques in Agdash, Diyally and Geokchai, have been handed over for schools, clubs, cinemas, Red Corners and reading huts.'[27]

However, progress was slow in many areas. In 1930 it was admitted that even three-quarters of the Communists in certain districts of Daghestan still observed religious rites.[28] In Ingushetia children refused to learn from books which they thought anti-religious; teachers even had to leave their schools for criticising Islam; party and Komsomol members, instead of working against Islam, themselves frequented the mosques.[29]

Ideological weapons were used to the full. 'Societies of the Godless' were set up in all Muslim areas, where they 'conducted mass agitation and undertook the publication in the native languages of anti-religious journals, books and popular brochures'. Mass anti-Islamic literature was also put out by the *Bezbozhnik* and *Ateist* publishing houses in Moscow as well as by the Press and scientific journals.

At first these efforts were hampered by the absence of a recognised party 'line' on Islam, beyond a general condemnation of it as reactionary. One theory about the origin of the Muslim faith put forward in the early 1930s suggested that it had begun as 'an ideology of the poor, the expression of the interests of the impoverished section of the people'. This theory was soon condemned as 'vicious' and as 'going against the basic

[71]

premises of Marxist teaching on the essence of religion in class society'.[30]

The 'triumph' of the opposed point of view 'which regards Islam as the ideology of a developing feudal system' was consolidated in 1935 when the article on Islam appeared in the *Bolshaya Sovetskaya Entsiklopediya*. This article described Islam as 'a fanatic reflection of social relations'; efforts were being made 'to adapt the feudal ideology and organisation of Islam to the new capitalist conditions'.[31] Within the USSR Islam had been used 'for the struggle against the Soviet régime'.[32] After the civil war 'Islam and its organisations continued to serve as rallying points for counter-revolutions'.[33] At present, it was said, 'counter-revolutionary elements, making use of the Koran, are trying to play on the religious feelings of believers, to hinder Socialist construction, to inflame national and religious hatred in order to break the united front of workers of the Soviet Union'.[34]

One of the authors of this article was L. Klimovich, who today occupies a place in relation to Islam similar to that of Oleshchuk in relation to Christianity. His pre-war output was typical. In 1928 he published a 'first attempt to expound the Koran with a revelation of its internal contradictions'.[35] His *Socialist Construction in the East and Religion* was 'one of the first attempts to generalise material on the execution of practical tasks of Socialist construction, cultural revolution and especially anti-religious propaganda in the Soviet East'.[36] In November, 1930, he addressed the Anti-Religious Section of the Institute of Philosophy of the Communist Academy on the subject 'Did Mohammed Exist?' He denied the 'historical reality of the person of Mohammed', describing him as an 'imaginary figure'. His address 'attracted much attention' and 'provided the impetus for further researches in this field'.[37] Next he put out *The Hajj—the Vampire of Islam*.[38] * His subsequent anti-Islamic efforts included an attack on the feast of *Kurban-Bairam* and an 'agitational notebook', *Against the Uraza*.[39] In 1936 his book *Islam in Tsarist Russia* appeared, and in 1937 a pamphlet for youth, *Concerning Islam*, devoted to 'unmasking the reactionary activity of the Muslim priesthood in the USSR from the first days of the Great October Socialist Revolution'.[40]

* The *Hajj*, the pilgrimage to Mecca, is the canonical obligation of every believer once in his life if he has the material means.

Soviet Muslims suffered severely in the Great Purge. The Godless leaders made free with such allegations as:

'The Muslim religious organisations and mosques . . . are centres of the activity of anti-Soviet, nationalist elements. The enemies of the people carry on their treacherous work under the flag of "defence of religion".'[41]

'On [Muslim] holidays and also during the performance of religious rites class enemies develop intensified counter-revolutionary activity.'[42]

'The activity of the counter-revolutionary Muslim priesthood in the USSR is directed by the Japanese secret service.'[43]

Pravda declared in the summer of 1937:

'A special place in the system of the Japanese secret service is occupied by the exploitation of counter-revolutionary bourgeois-nationalist Muslim elements. Aiming to organise mass diversions in the deep rear of the USSR (Central Asia, the Urals, Tataria) . . . the Japanese openly support the leaders of the counter-revolutionary Muslim emigration. In Japan the chief organiser of espionage and diversionary work "on the Muslim line" is the mullah Kurban-galiev, who long ago entered the service of the Japanese Intelligence.'[44]

Samursky, head of both the Communist Party and the Soviet Government of Daghestan, who had done his best to eliminate Islam in the area, was shot in 1937 as one who 'helped the mullahs to agitate against the collective farms, took care that the population should observe religious rites, and in every way hindered the development of anti-religious propaganda'.[45]

Many Muslim religious leaders were accused of sabotaging the railways.[46] A number of mullahs were imprisoned for practising ritual circumcision which was equated with criminal mutilation. But late in 1938, when anti-religious violence was called off in view of the imminence of war, they were released on the ground that circumcision had never been forbidden by law.[47]

1939–1947

By the time war broke out Soviet Islam was in a much weakened state. In the whole of the USSR there were only 1,312 mosques served by 8,052 mullahs.[48] The *medresseh*, the Islamic academies, had all been 'liquidated' by 1938.[49] As for the *Shari'ah*, as long ago as 1933 it had been denounced as a 'tool of the enemies of Socialist construction', which, as a result

[73]

of 'decisive struggle', by the Soviet Government, 'has now ceased to exist in the USSR'.[50]

On July 18, 1941, the Central Muslim Religious Board in Ufa, the governing body of Soviet Islam,[51] summoned the faithful 'to rise up in defence of their native land, to pray in the mosques for the victory of the Red Army and to give their blessing to their sons, fighting for a just cause'. On September 2, Mufti Abdurakhman Rassulev, the head of the Board, again called on Soviet Muslims 'to defend our country in the name of religion and to appeal to all our brother Muslims to do the same', and concluded: 'In mosques and in private pray to Allah to help defeat the enemy of the Red Army'.

This support did not go unrewarded. A representative conference of the heads of Soviet Islam was permitted to meet at Ufa in May, 1942.[52] A Central Asian Muslim conference was held at Tashkent in October, 1943,[53] and another, of Transcaucasian Muslim leaders, at Baku in May, 1944.[54] Important changes in Muslim ecclesiastical organisation were sanctioned. The former Central Board at Ufa was replaced by four regional Boards:

> Central Asia and Kazakhstan (in Tashkent);
> European part of the USSR and Siberia (in Ufa);
> North Caucasus (in Buynaksk);
> Transcaucasia (in Baku);[55]

Working in co-ordination with the governmental Council for the Affairs of Religious Cults, the Boards have been said to be concerned with the opening of new mosques 'where the need for them exists', the appointment of mullahs and muezzins and the training of religious leaders.[56]

The re-opening of a number of mosques was permitted. In December, 1944, the Mufti of Ufa said that 10 mosques had been opened in Gorki, Omsk, Novosibirsk and other towns, while others were to be opened in Chkalov, Chelyabinsk and elsewhere.[57] In October, 1947, I. V. Polyanksy, Chairman of the Council for Affairs of Religious Cults, said there were 3,000 mosques in the Soviet Union.[58]

In 1945 a group of Soviet Muslims was permitted to perform the *Hajj*. Facilities, including aircraft, were provided by the Soviet Government.

A further *Hajj* was apparently planned for the following year. In 1950 Mufti Ishan Babakhan told the visiting French General

[74]

Tubert that in 1946 he received 200 applications from the faithful of Central Asia and Kazakhstan. Since most of the applicants were allegedly too old and destitute, he forwarded only 17 names to the Council for Religious Cults, which approved them but was 'unable to obtain visas from the governments concerned'—those of Iran and the Hedjaz.[59] A similar story is told of 1947, when Mufti Ishan Babakhan forwarded 40 applications which were approved by the Council. Again, according to the Mufti, 'two governments which call themselves Muslim, those of Turkey and Iran, refused us transit visas'.[60] But at an earlier date the cholera epidemic in the Middle East was officially given as the reason for the abandonment of the 1947 Hajj.[61]

1948-1966

Since 1948 the position of Soviet Islam has been similar to that of the Russian Orthodox Church. On the one hand the Soviet Communist Party has sought to eradicate this faith in campaigns of varying intensity. On the other hand the Muslim leaders have judged it expedient to give full support to Soviet policies as the price for the continued existence of their institutions. The present Chief Mufti of Central Asia and Kazakhstan, Zia al-Din Babakhanov, who succeeded his father in 1957, declared in November, 1952, in a broadcast to Muslims in the Middle East:

'As a Muslim I call on you to support the resolutions [of the World Peace Congress] on the need for the unification of Germany, to support the cause of peace, backing the Japanese people in their struggle against the San Francisco Treaty imposed on them by the USA. I fully endorse the resolutions of the Peking Peace Conference on Korea where the American aggressors under the banner of the UN are exterminating towns, villages and peoples by the use of gas and germ bombs. . . . If the peoples do not take up the cause of peace today, what is happening in Korea will happen in these countries also. I call upon the peoples of the East to prepare for the Vienna Peace Congress.'[62]

In October, 1960, Babakhanov supported the Soviet Government's campaign against the UN operations in the Congo and told a meeting of the Soviet Afro-Asian Solidarity Committee:

'The Muslims in the USSR pour scorn on the actions of the imperialist aggressors in the Congo Republic. The peoples of Asia and Africa must see to it that the imperialists, headed by the American

[75]

neo-colonisers, leave the Congo immediately and give its people a real opportunity to settle their fate themselves.'[63]

The concessions won by this support have been relatively minor. In 1948 Islamic theological training was allowed to be resumed with the founding of the Mir-i- Arab *medresseh* in Bokhara. The Barak Khan *medresseh* in Tashkent, which was provided for in the same year, finally opened in 1956. In 1955 three graduates from the Mir-i- Arab *medresseh* were admitted to the Muslim University of El Azhar in Cairo[64] and others have followed.

However, the resumption of Islamic theological training has been on a small scale. In 1953–54 the Mir-i- Arab *medresseh*, which has 50 *hujra* (cells), had 100 students and must have reached its maximum in 1956 when it had a complement of 105.[65] Since then its numbers appear to have declined considerably. In 1962 it had less than 50 students. The numbers at the Barak Khan *medresseh* are reputedly even lower.

Thus there is obvious substance in a complaint made by *Nauka i Religiya* that of Muslim religious leaders in the Soviet Union 'only a few graduate from the Bokhara and Tashkent *medresseh*', although the subsequent contention that 'the rest are impostors attracted by an easy life'[66] reflects customary Soviet hostility towards the Muslim priesthood. In 1957 the Turkmenian First Party Secretary deplored that it was 'precisely the low level of anti-religious propaganda and all our ideological work among youth' which explained the fact that 'some people in our Soviet school go to study in Muslim theological training establishments'.[67] In 1964 the establishment of an underground *medresseh* at No. 117, Altynkyulskaya Street, in the town of Andizhan, was denounced. This *medresseh*, unlike those at Bokhara and Tashkent which cater only for students over the age of 20, had set out to teach children verses from the Koran and Muslim prayers and had encouraged them to recite these among their schoolmates.[68]

Publication of Muslim literature has also been on a very restricted scale. In 1948, for the first time since the October Revolution, permission was given to publish an edition of the Koran[69] and since then a number of small editions have appeared. Otherwise Muslim publications seem to have been confined to a few books and religious calendars. In 1957 *Knizhnaya Letopis* (The Book Chronicle), a journal 'in which the books and brochures coming out in the USSR in all languages and in all branches of knowledge are registered',[70] mentioned a book called *Islam [i Musulmanskoye] Bogosluzhenie* (Islam [and Muslim] Forms of Service) by the Head of the Spiritual Board for European Russia and Siberia, as having come out in that year, and as having included 69 pages of text in Kazan Tatar in Arabic characters.[71] In 1958 the same source gave the information that the Board for Central Asia and Kazakhstan had put out a 12-page calendar written in Uzbek in Arabic characters, with a circulation of 10,000 copies.[72] In 1963, however, *Knizhnaya Letopis* did not mention the publication of a single Muslim book or calendar.

Since 1953 another limited concession has been the renewal of permission for small groups of Soviet Muslims to make the *Hajj* to Mecca. But while maximum publicity has been given to these pilgrimages for the benefit of Muslims abroad, it has had no softening effect on the Party's attitude to Islam in the USSR. This was demonstrated with particular force in 1954. On August 2 *Tass* announced that 21 Soviet Muslims would be allowed to visit Mecca in two groups. The parties travelled in official aircraft under special arrangements made by the Soviet Government. Official Press conferences were arranged at the time of their departure from Moscow and on their return on August 30. In broadcasts abroad there were frequent allusions to the freedom of worship afforded to Soviet Muslims, and on August 14 *Tass* reported that the pilgrims had expressed their gratitude 'for being granted the opportunity to carry out their sacred rites'.

Inside the USSR, however, the propaganda campaign against Islam continued. On August 12 *Ashkhabad Radio* broadcast an attack on the 'reactionary rôle of Islam' to Turkmenians. A week later at the Third Congress of Soviet Writers of Tadzhikistan, B. G. Gafurov, then First Party Secretary in Tadzhikistan,* denounced religious survivals as impeding the movement towards Communism and declared:

'These circumstances oblige our writers to unmask the reactionary rôle of religion mercilessly, to conduct propaganda for the atheistic and materialist world outlook and to write humorous and satirical works ridiculing the machinations of the clergy. Every tenet of religion is anti-scientific and absurd, a fact which offers

* Gafurov was appointed Director of the Institute of Oriental Studies of the USSR Academy of Sciences in 1956. In 1961 this institute was renamed the Peoples of Asia Institute.

unlimited possibilities for unmasking it and making it ridiculous in the eyes of the workers.'[73]

Since 1957–58 Muslims have been exposed to most of the forms of anti-religious work which characterised the Party's intensified campaign against religious belief. The Atheist Club formed early in 1960 in the Historical Faculty of the Central Asian University in Tashkent,[74] for example, is only one of many specialised institutions since set up as focal points for atheistic propaganda in Muslim areas.

Anti-Islamic propaganda has also made use of the Soviet cosmonauts. In May, 1961, Professor Klimovich published an article drawing an unfavourable comparison between Mohammed's night ride to the Seventh Heaven and Gagarin's orbit of the earth.[75] In May, 1962, the story was told of how an Arab intellectual had shown that Gagarin's exploit had destroyed his faith and his trust in the Koran.[76]

Anti-Muslim entertainment has included the 'documentary' film *Shadows from the Past* issued by Tadzhikfilm in 1963, which depicts the rogueries of a fake healer who lives sumptuously off the alms of the faithful,[77] a 1963 play *The Corpses*, in which the author 'tears the mask from the hypocritical Muslim clergy and from the igorant and fanatical society of an out-of-the-way Azerbaidzhan town at the end of the last century'[78]; and a musical comedy *Tashbalta in Love*, staged in the Mukimi Theatre in Tashkent in 1962, of which it was said that 'under such a hail of witticisms and gibes even the most inveterate fanatic would turn into an atheist'.[79]

Statements by apostates and trials of mullahs to discredit Muslim religious leaders have also been exploited. In 1960, for example, Pir Niyaz Khodzha, a reputed 22nd descendant of Mohammed, publicly named a number of fellow mullahs and ishans as 'parasites, adventurers, idlers and profligates'[80] and the trial in Kirghizia of a mullah charged with minor assault was used to 'open the eyes of many to the activities of the "servants of Allah"' and to portray them as 'inveterate grabbers and parasites'.[81]

There have been reports of the closing of large numbers of mosques 'at the request of believers'[82] and determined efforts have been made to curb pilgrimages to holy places, which are particularly well supported in Central Asia and Azerbaidzhan. In November, 1963, it was stated that as a result of 'individual atheistic work' pilgrimages to Kunamli in the Bairam-Ali production directorate in Turkmenia had finally been stopped.[83] Earlier a campaign had been directed against pilgrimages to the 'Takht-i-Sulayman' ('Throne of Solomon') mountain near the town of Osh in Kirghizia. Here, after some 15,000 people had been organised to protest against these pilgrimages, the Executive Committee of the Osh Town Soviet passed a resolution to ban them and to convert the 'white house' on the mountain into a museum.[84] In January, 1962, however, the complaint was made that 'the local Soviets here issued resolutions forbidding pilgrimages, but this has not changed anything'. About 400 people were visiting the 'Takht-i-Sulayman' mountain between seven and ten in the morning, and the number was greater in the afternoon.[85]

Reports of such passive resistance are not uncommon and it seems that, at least in many rural areas, the Party's anti-religious campaign has driven Islam underground rather than reduced its influence. In September, 1963, *Nauka i Religiya* complained that although 'according to official data there are in Tadzhikistan no more than 18 registered mosques and 69 priests', in fact 'scarcely a collective farm or *Kishlak* [village] will be found in the Republic, where there is not a mosque existing under the guise of a tea-room or restaurant'.[86]

The journal also deplored the presence of schoolchildren, teachers and even Party members among 'the very many inhabitants of Tadzhikistan' who had observed the Uraza fast from January 26 to February 25, 1963.[87] In January, 1966, it described how atheist teachers in a Cherkessian village combat the observance of this fast, said to be 'one of the extremely widespread survivals of Islam'. From the absence of smoke over a *saklia* (Caucasian dwelling), they know that people are fasting there. That is a signal for them to take measures to prevent the believing parents and grandparents from starving the children and forcing them to observe Uraza.[88]

In April, 1965, a museum of atheism was opened in an ancient mosque at the tomb of Bakhauddin, near Bokhara, in Uzbekistan. Formerly the holy sheikh was so revered throughout the area that a pilgrimage to his tomb was considered by believers 'equivalent to the pilgrimage to Mecca'.[89] A 'miraculous spring' on the outskirts of the town of Nurata was also reported to have become a centre for anti-religious propaganda, where doctors, teachers and agronomists explained to believers their delusions.[90] Anti-religious museums have also been created in several other Central Asian 'holy places'.[91]

The continuing loyalty to Islam on the part of local officials seems to be a major factor in preventing the anti-religious campaign from achieving real impact in many Muslim areas.

On July 4, 1963, The First Party Secretary in Azerbaidzhan complained that Party members and Komsomols had taken part in the great day of mourning of the Shiite Muslims, the tenth day of the Muslim month of Moharram, when the faithful commemorate the chief martyrs of the Shiah faith.[92] The following month three Communists were expelled from the Kazakhstan Party for assisting in the building of a *mazar* (mausoleum).[93] In September, 1963, the case was raised of Party members in the Andizhan area of Uzbekistan, who were observing religious ceremonies and attending Muslim prayer meetings.[94] In November, 1963, Ilichev, the Chairman of the Party Central Committee's Ideological Commission, revealed that in Tadzhikistan, not only were Muslim services being held outside mosques, in private houses and apartments but that 'however astounding this may be, certain Muslim ceremonies have been conducted in the presence of representatives of the local authorities'.[95] In October, 1964, *Pravda Vostoka* announced the dismissal of the Minister of Trade of the Kara-Kalpak ASSR, whose observance of Muslim rites had been reported in the newspaper in July.[96]

Meanwhile there has been evidence of the continuing strength of Islam. Ilichev described how a 70-year-old collective farmer, after failing to get written permission from his local Muslim leaders not to observe the Uraza fast, had written to Tadzhikistan's Council of Ministers so as to be able to meet the pressure of public opinion.[97] In January, 1964, it was revealed that in Kazakhstan the mosque in the town of Kentau had in 1963 received half as much again in offerings as it had in 1962, and that 'hundreds of young men and women' had visited the Chimkent mosque during the festival of Kurban-bairam.[98]

Nauka i Religiya has repeatedly expressed concern at the tenacious survival of Muslim customs and the 'anti-scientific and very harmful tendency' to identify them with national characteristics and traditions.[99] The prevalence of this 'erroneous' view among young people 'including the intelligentsia' in Tashkent, despite the militancy of atheist work there,[100] was described in May, 1966. Among 210 people who observed the *nikokh* (marriage) ritual in the Oktyabr *raion* in Tashkent, there were 16 scientific workers, students and research students, 14 teachers in higher educational establishments and schools, seven engineers and agronomists and seven doctors and medical workers.[101]

(b) CATHOLICISM

In Imperial Russia the Roman Catholic Church had few adherents among ethnic Russians,[102] its following consisting mainly of people of Polish or Lithuanian descent;[103] there were also Catholics of two Oriental rites (Uniats). They were persecuted, often savagely. In 1842 Pope Gregory XVI called the attention of the world's Catholics to 'the painful oppression to which Catholicism is subjected in Russia'.[104] The edict of religious toleration of 1905 resulted in a large increase in the number of Catholics until in 1912 they totalled 11,000,000.[105] The few Catholics left within the USSR after the settlement of its Western frontiers in the early 1920s belonged to three rites —the Latin rite centred upon the Metropolitan Archdiocese of Mogilev,[106] the Armenian rite centred on the Latin diocese of Tiraspol,[107] and the Byzantine-Slav rite with its Latin Archdiocese in Mogilev.[108]

Implacable Bolshevik hostility towards Catholicism was inevitable since, like Islam, it represented part of a movement outside their control. Relations were strained from the first. The clergy were bold in the defence of their Church and refused to accept the decree of January, 1918, making churches public property and forbidding religious instruction of children.[109] With the approval of Mgr. de Ropp, Archbishop of Mogilev since July, 1917,[110] Mgr. Budkiewicz, Dean of the Roman Catholic clergy in Petrograd, issued an Instruction early in December, 1918, laying down that Church property should not be surrendered until actually requisitioned and every effort should be made to save it.[111]

The Communists arrested Mgr. de Ropp. Sentenced to death, he was later expelled from the country[112] and lived an exile in Warsaw until his death in July, 1939.[113] His Auxiliary, Mgr. Cepliak, titular Bishop of Evaria and suffragan of Mogilev, was promoted titular Archbishop of Acrida on March 28, 1919.[114] In a circular of September 12 he warned that to make contracts concerning Church property without the permission of the ecclesiastical authorities was 'equivalent to appropriating it and handing it over to illegal hands' and was 'a profanation' in which Catholics could take not part. The Archbishop had already protested against its nationalisation and declared that 'parishioners are obliged on their part to repeat the protest'.[115]

The crisis came over the confiscation of Church valuables for famine relief, ordered by the decree of February 23, 1922. The immediate consequence was the arrest, trial and condemnation of many Catholic churchmen, culminating in the arrest of Mgr. Cepliak, Mgr. Budkiewicz, Mgr. Fedorov, Exarch of the Catholics of the Byzantine rite in Moscow,[116] and others. In March, 1923, the Archbishop, 14 priests and one layman were tried, charges of treasonable relations with the Polish Government being added to those of opposition to the Soviet Government's anti-religious measures.[117] The defendants declared that as the sacred vessels belonged to the Church, they could not surrender them without Papal permission; and that they must continue to teach the Catechism since no legislation could supersede the natural law commanding priests to enlighten children.[118] Mgr. Cepliak maintained that the Revolution had set the Catholics free and that the idea of counter-revolution had not entered their heads.[119] The Archbishop and Mgr. Budkiewicz were sentenced to death,[120] and the rest imprisoned. Only Mgr. Budkiewicz was executed.[121]; Mgr. Cepliak's sentence was commuted to life imprisonment; eventually his release was obtained under a Russo-Polish agreement to exchange prisoners and he followed his superior to Poland, where he received the See of Vilna in December, 1925.[122]

The Communists next severed the last link between Soviet Catholics and the Vatican. In 1922 a Papal mission for famine relief had been admitted. From the first its efforts were played down; today these efforts are described as 'of course, negligible', designed only to ensure that 'the authorities' suspicions should not be aroused as to the real intentions and aims of the Papal mission'. A whispering campaign began that the 'impudent Jesuits' had 'established links with the internal counter-revolution, disseminated provocatory rumours, recruited spies and spied themselves'. The recall of Mgr. Walsh, the leader of the mission, was demanded. His successor allegedly 'intensified still further the hostile activities of the Vatican mission'. In 1924 the whole mission was expelled.[123]

In 1925, the Bolsheviks, then eager to gain international

respectability, entered into negotiations with the Vatican for a concordat on the questions of education, finance, the appointment of Catholic bishops, the publication of Papal Bulls and free communication between the Vatican and Soviet Catholics.[124] A leading Jesuit, Mgr. d'Herbigny, visited Moscow and the following year returned under the auspices of the French Ambassador to reorganise the Catholic Church.[125] Mgr. d'Herbigny succeeded in consecrating four titular bishops and appointing them and other priests to be Apostolic Administrators in the dioceses before he was expelled.[126]

The Soviet Government broke off the negotiations for a concordat.[127] The newly-consecrated bishops were quickly accused of having 'fallen into counter-revolution'[128] and those subsequently put on trial included 11 Apostolic Administrators.

But the entire Catholic clergy was involved. Already in 1926 a 'Polish spy' tried at Kharkov 'confessed' to having entered the service of Polish Intelligence on the advice of a priest and to having been assisted in her work by priests both in Poland and in the Ukraine. In August priests were tried at Korosten (Ukraine) on charges of being agents of Polish Intelligence and smuggling in Polish spies.[129] Similar trials followed throughout the Ukraine.[130]

Some individual churches remained with a number of priests to serve them.[131] The official campaign against Catholicism was therefore not abandoned.

The most bitter of the anti-religious propaganda of the mid-1930s was directed against Catholicism and the Pope.[132] Violent persecution was resumed. In 1937 organs of the NKVD 'revealed and destroyed not a few nests of spies directed by "holy" Catholic priests'. Many priests were charged with being spies and agents of foreign States and with organising gangs to blow up factories, wreck bridges and railways, disrupt the collective farms, etc.[133]

Several million Catholics came under Soviet rule when Eastern Poland and the Baltic States were occupied in 1939–40. Many of these were Uniats of the Greek-Ruthenian rite dating from the Union of Brest of 1596 whereby a sizeable Orthodox group then under Polish rule accepted Papal authority while retaining their Orthodox rites and practices.[134]

Soon the Communists moved against the Uniat Church. On October 10, 1939, the aged Mgr. Szeptycky, Uniat Metropolitan of Lvov, wrote to the Holy See:

'The parishes are at the mercy of local committees . . . The monasteries seem doomed to inevitable suppression . . . The churches are confiscated and occupied. Catholic schools are closed.'

He asked to be given a Coadjutor with right of succession and concluded:

'I humbly beg the Holy Father to give me His Apostolic and Fatherly blessing and to designate, delegate and appoint me to die for the Faith and the Church. We all understand our duty.'[135]

In response to his request Mgr. Slipy, Rector of the Theological Academy at Lvov, was nominated as his Coadjutor; on December 22 the Metropolitan consecrated him titular Archbishop of Serre.[136]

The Communists then attempted to oust the Metropolitan. They offered his office to Dr. Gavril Kostelnik, director of the ecclesiastical review *Nyva*, who indignantly rejected it. Thereupon they arrested his 17-year-old son and repeated their offer. Dr. Kostelnik was interviewed many times by the NKVD, who warned him that his son's fate depended on his decision. The German invasion brought these interviews to an end; but Dr. Kostelnik's son was never seen again.[137] Describing the Soviet occupation, Metropolitan Szeptycky wrote:

'The number of priests murdered, or imprisoned in circumstances which make it probable that they are dead, is 11 or 12 in my diocese, and 20 in the diocese of Przemysl. The priests imprisoned or deported from my diocese number 33.'[138]

In the Baltic States, particularly Lithuania where 81·2 per cent of the population were Roman Catholics, the situation was equally bad. Immediately after the Soviet occupation in June, 1940, the puppet Soviet Government of Lithuania unilaterally abolished the concordat with the Holy See and expelled the Papal Nuncio.[139] On July 1 the withdrawal of State support from all religious institutions was decreed. One by one the Catholic seminaries were reduced to impotence by the requisitioning of their premises for the Red Army and the Communist Party. When on January 14, 1941, Bishops Borisevicius and Brizgys protested to Pozdnyakov, the Kremlin's representative and real ruler of Lithuania, he told them that what had been done in Soviet Russia in 20 years was to be achieved in Soviet Lithuania in two to three years.[140] Measures were taken to prevent all religious instruction of the young. In April, 1941, instructions went out from Kaunas that all priests must sign a form stating:

'I have been strictly forbidden and have no right to teach religion to children of school age, either in schools or in my home or in any place in general. Thus I have no right whatsoever to talk to them about religious matters. I have been informed I will be held responsible for failure to comply with this warning.'[141]

The Catholic clergy was closely watched;[142] and in the year or so of Soviet occupation 42 priests were arrested.[143]

By August, 1941, the Soviet Union had only 1,744 Catholic churches served by 2,309 priests.[144] Soviet Catholics could play little or no part in the Second World War since nearly all of them were under German occupation within a few weeks. For those who remained under Soviet rule the war years brought a degree of toleration. In Moscow permission was given for the French Catholic Church to be placed at the disposal of all the city's Catholics;[145] apparently 15 priests were available to minister to them.[146]

With the end of the war the campaign against the Catholic Church was resumed. In 1946 two of the three Catholic seminaries were closed down.[147] (In 1959 a Soviet standard reference gave the information that the Catholic Church had two seminaries, in Kaunas and Riga.[148])

The Catholic Church in Lithuania survived not only violent persecution but also the threat of a State-sponsored 'national church'. Lithuanian émigrés report that during March–April, 1952, representatives of the clergy were summoned four times to the Central Committee of the Lithuanian Communist Party where pressure was exerted on them to consent to the establishment of a 'National Lithuanian Catholic Church'.[149] They withstood this pressure and no such church has materialised.

Part of the price of survival has been the Catholic leaders' public support for Soviet foreign policies and objectives and the 'peace' campaign. In October, 1950, Canon Stankevicius declared at the Second All-Union Peace Conference in Moscow:

'We Catholics of Lithuania . . . urge all Christians to condemn those who are committing a crime against Christian morals and against humanity. . . . That is why we denounce the American and British invaders who have kindled the fire of a new bloody war in Korea. . . . Hypocritical are the assertions that America and Britain are now democratic countries. Any country that seeks to enslave others and encourage racial discrimination is not a democracy but a land of tyranny. We pray for peace every day and we call upon all believers to offset the danger of a new war through joint efforts.'[150]

A year later in Latvia Bishop Strods publicly stated that:

'The self-seeking capitalists of America and Britain, together with the revanchists of Western Germany and Japan, are trying to unleash war. They are preparing it first and foremost against our State—the Soviet Union. Most probably this war would already have begun if the fighters for peace throughout the world, headed by the Soviet Union, had not given an energetic rebuff to the war-mongers and if atomic energy and the atomic weapon had remained a monopoly of the aggressor.'[151]

In contrast the entire Greek-Ruthenian or Ukrainian Catholic Uniat Church was destroyed in the latter 1940s. The Western Ukraine was reoccupied by Soviet troops in July–August, 1944. At first the Communists' attitude seemed quite different from that of 1939–41. Churches were reopened; seminaries and convents were allowed to continue; soldiers and officers openly attended services; and hostile propaganda was imperceptible.[152] On November 1 the Metropolitan died, aged 79, having governed the see for 44 years.[153] Mgr. Slipy, his Coadjutor, succeeded him.

The position of the Uniat Church now began to deteriorate. In the autumn and winter of 1944 the Soviet authorities summoned the clergy to regional meetings where they had to listen to speakers disparaging the history of the Church, the Papacy and Roman Catholicism.[154] As a conciliatory gesture and in the hope of obtaining a *modus vivendi* Metropolitan Slipy sent 100,000 roubles for the war wounded to Moscow by a special commission headed by Father Kostelnik. The commission was coldly received; it was told that the Church would be protected only if it helped in suppressing the Ukrainian anti-Soviet partisan movement.[155] Metropolitan Slipy replied by repeatedly reminding the clergy and faithful of the obligations imposed by the Fifth Commandment; but his exhortations were considered insufficient.[156] The destruction of the Uniat Church was put in hand.

On April 11, Mgr. Slipy, Mgr. Budka, his Vicar General, Mgr. Charnetski, Apostolic Visitor for Volhynia, Mgr. Chomyszyn, Bishop of Stanislav, and Mgr. Latysevsky, his Auxiliary, were arrested.[157] A few days later 500 priests were arrested and deported to Russia.[158] The students of two seminaries (Lvov and Stanislav) were conscripted for military service. For 10 consecutive days the police searched the Cathedral of St. George and the Archbishop's Palace in Lvov and carried off the archives, many religious objects and furniture. A similar search was made of the Bishop's Palace at Stanislav.[159]

The arrested hierarchs were kept in prison for nearly a year without trial. Then on March 1, 1946, an indictment was published by the Ukrainian Procurator accusing them of traitorous activity and collaboration with the German occupation forces.[160] 'Documents' were adduced to prove their 'criminal complicity' with the 'German Fascist occupier', particularly the Gestapo, the police and the intelligence service. They were also accused of sending Ukrainians to forced labour in Germany. To these charges they allegedly pleaded guilty. The trial took place behind closed doors—not in Lvov, but in Kiev. The 80-year-old Mgr. Chomyszyn was sentenced to 10 years' forced labour but died in a Kiev prison in January, 1947. Mgr. Slipy, Mgr. Budka and Mgr. Latysevsky were condemned to eight years' forced labour and Mgr. Charnetski, 'an agent of the Vatican', to five years.[161] A German ex-prisoner of war who returned from Russia in 1954 reported that on the expiry of his sentence Mgr. Slipy was sentenced to a further 17 years' forced labour.[162]

Because his residence was outside the Soviet Union the Bishop of Przemysl, Mgr. Kocylovsky, remained at liberty for a while. But already in September, 1944, it had been agreed between the Soviet Union and the satellite Polish administration that Ukrainians living in Poland should be deported to the Soviet Ukraine. On September 21, 1945, Mgr. Kocylovsky was arrested. Foreseeing this, he had written:

'In case of my arrest and deportation, I humbly beg to notify the Holy Father that I place before Him my vow of fidelity and absolute devotion until my last breath, last beat of my heart, asking for His paternal blessing.'[163]

In prison he was instructed to declare that he was ready to be 'repatriated'. But he replied that he and his clergy were bound to the See of Przemysl and only the Pope could release them from this obligation. After two months' imprisonment he was handed over to the Soviet police and on January 8, 1946, transferred to Soviet territory. The NKVD tried to persuade him to abandon Rome. These efforts proved futile, and on

January 24 he was permitted to return to Przemysl. There he was continually spied on until, on June 25, he was again arrested, handed over to the Soviet police and imprisoned, first in Lvov, then in Kiev. Finally he was confined in a home for the aged where he died on November 17, 1947.[164]

On June 26, 1946, Mgr. Lakota, titular Bishop of Daonio and Auxiliary of Przemysl, was arrested with the whole Chapter and transported to Lvov, then to Kiev. From here they were thought to have been deported to Northern Russia to join Metropolitan Slipy and the other Ukrainian Catholic hierarchs.[165]

After the first arrests in 1945, several Canons elected at Lvov a Vicar Capitular; but he was soon arrested.[166] The Deans were forbidden to issue any orders; and only those priests were allowed to officiate who were registered with the authorities. At the same time an 'Initiative Group for the Reunion of the Greek-Catholic Church of Galicia with the Russian Orthodox Church' appeared, headed by Dr. Kostelnik.[167] The Ukrainian Catholic clergy in exile have described him as very energetic and a capable organiser, enjoying great authority as an ardent patriot and man of learning, but at the same time a priest who performed his duties mechanically and would compromise to keep out of trouble. They recall the attempts to seduce him during the first Soviet occupation. In 1945 these attempts succeeded: two of his sons had fought with the Germans and he and his family were therefore liable to deportation to Siberia. To save them he consented to organise the 'Initiative Group'.[168]

He was assisted by two other Uniat priests, Melnik of the Diocese of Przemysl and Pelvetsky of the Diocese of Stanislav.[169] They held conferences, wrote anti-Vatican propaganda and threatened with loss of their parishes and deportation those who resisted them.[170] On May 28 they appealed to the whole Uniat clergy to join them. Four days later over 300 priests protested to Molotov:

'After the arrest of the entire Episcopate and a great number of priests of the Catholic Church and in consequence of the prohibition to elect a member of the Catholic clergy as our head, our Church finds itself in a very abnormal situation ... We do not want to meddle with what is called politics but only to dedicate ourselves entirely to the salvation of the souls of our brethren and our own ... Our attitude towards the work of Father Kostelnik is completely negative. We condemn his activity as harmful, as absolutely opposed to the tradition of the Church and contrary to the truth proclaimed by Christ ... We cannot listen to a voice inciting to apostasy from the Faith.

'We ask our Government therefore to liberate our Bishops, beginning with our Metropolitan. While awaiting this liberation ... we ask that a canonically legal organ may administer the whole ecclesiastical province of Lvov. We want to believe that the Government will receive our request and will come to our aid, since the Stalin Constitution guarantees to all citizens, and therefore to us also, freedom of conscience and of religious worship.'[171]

This protest was in vain. On June 18 the Ukrainian Council of People's Commissars, of which Khrushchev was chairman, formally recognised the 'Initiative Group' as the temporary administrative organ for the direction of the Ukrainian Catholic Church and authorised it to regulate the administration of parishes and their reunion with the Orthodox Church. The 'Initiative Group' was instructed to submit a list of all priests and superiors of monasteries who refused to submit to its jurisdiction.[172] The obdurate were then interviewed by the NKVD and given two documents to sign, one consenting to join the 'Initiative Group', the other testifying to their freedom of choice. Continued refusal meant arrest. By 1946 about 800 Ukrainian Catholic priests were in prison, including 500 from the Archdiocese of Lvov.[173]

Some churches were closed and many convents suppressed.[174] The ecclesiastical boundaries were modified. The Archdiocese of Lvov became a simple Diocese and the Orthodox Bishop Makarii took up residence in the Metropolitan's Palace. The Diocese of Przemysl was replaced by that of Sambor-Drogobych.[175] Kostelnik, Pelvetsky and Melnik made a preliminary visit to Kiev and were interviewed by Metropolitan Ioann, Orthodox Exarch of the Ukraine.[176] On February 20, 1946, they returned 'with the first group of Uniat priests for reunification'. At a ceremony in the Kiev-Pechersk monastery Kostelnik declared: 'The yoke imposed on the Galician people by the Roman Popes is now being removed.' His two chief collaborators received the tonsure and were made Orthodox bishops, Pelvetsky as Antonii of Stanislav and Melnik as Mikhail of Sambor-Drogobych.[177]

They hastened back to Lvov and summoned a *Sobor* (Council). Only 204 priests and 12 laymen attended the meetings held on March 8 in the Cathedral of St. George under the chairmanship of Kostelnik and in the presence of the new Bishops Antonii and Mikhail and also the Orthodox Bishops Makarii and Nestor, attended by the Exarch Ioann's chief administrator, Father Ruzhitsky.[178] Kostelnik declared that the Uniats had 'wrongly retained bad seeds of faith received from the Roman Popes who worked always with violence, cunning, deceit, trampling on the sacred truth in the name of their love of power and their satanic pride'.[179]

Kostelnik then proposed to liquidate the Union of 1596, to break with Rome, to return to Orthodoxy, to rejoin the Russian Orthodox Church.[180] His proposals were adopted by the *Sobor*, which added:

'The Vatican was completely on the side of bloody Fascism and came out against the Soviet Union, which . . . saved our Ukrainian people from slavery and destruction and united all our lands . . . thus liberating us from national and religious oppression.'[181]

A message was sent to Patriarch Aleksei requesting him to 'receive us into the bosom of the All-Russian Orthodox Catholic Church',[182] and another to the Oecumenical Patriarch of Constantinople informing him of the *Sobor*'s decisions.[183] The Presidium of the *Sobor* (Kostelnik, Melnik and Pelvetsky) also sent a telegram to Stalin expressing 'the most profound gratitude for Your great deed—the gathering into one of the Ukrainian lands without which it would have been impossible even to dream of liquidating our religious separation';[184] and another to Khrushchev, thanking him 'for Your wise leadership as Head of the Government of our Motherland—the Great Ukrainian Soviet State'.[185] Finally the Presidium addressed the clergy and faithful, instructing them that 'Uniats in assimilating Romish views and tendencies condemn themselves to poverty, renouncing their own spiritual treasures', and 'summoning you all, priests and faithful, to hear our voice and accept our decision'.[186]

On March 9, in St. George's Cathedral, the 204 priests 'renounced the Romish errors' and the reunification was completed. The Exarch, Metropolitan Ioann, gave an address and read a message from Patriarch Aleksei. Then Father Ruzhitsky read a report on the Russian Orthodox Church 'in its struggle for Holy Orthodoxy'.[187]

On April 4 Kostelnik, Melnik and Pelvetsky flew to Moscow where they were received by G. F. Utkin, a member of the Government's Council for the Affairs of the Russian Orthodox

Church. They were subsequently received by the Patriarch, accompanied by Karpov, the Council's Chairman. On April 8 the Council itself gave a reception for the visitors at which Karpov spoke. He saw them again before they left for Lvov on April 10.[188]

Shortly afterwards Bishop Makarii of Lvov published a list of Ukrainian Catholic priests who had accepted the decisions of the Sobor; 1,111 were named out of a total of 2,303, but the list contained the names of some already dead.[189]

The end of Kostelnik indicates the intense opposition to his work. In the months following the *Sobor* he 'carried on intense work to confirm and spread the great cause' and 'no one so skilfully refuted the lying proofs of the Latin hypocrites'.[190] The anti-Vatican resolution adopted by the Moscow Conference of Autocephalous Orthodox Churches in the summer of 1948 was his handiwork.[191] On September 20 he was murdered in Lvov, allegedly by an 'agent of the Vatican'.[192] The Ukrainian Catholics in Rome declare that the assassins were Ukrainian partisans.[193]

For a while the Greek-Ruthenian Diocese of Mukachevo, dating from 1771, survived in the Carpatho-Ukraine. On October 27, 1944, Soviet forces entered Uzhgorod, the seat of the 33-year-old Bishop, Mgr. Romza. At first any attack on the Church was avoided. The military commander assured Mgr. Romza of his goodwill and invited him to speak on the anniversary of the October Revolution. As a gesture the Bishop complied and briefly exhorted the people to welcome the liberators and to pray for peace. But the published version of his address was so distorted that he protested, only to be told that the authorities had published what he should have said in accordance with their directive.[194]

Then, because he would not make a declaration denying the existence of religious persecution in the Soviet Union, Mgr. Romza began to be labelled a Fascist and an enemy of the Soviet people while anti-Catholic propaganda greatly increased. The Bishop was summoned before the Soviet political representative, General Mekhlis, who asserted that although some kind of religion was necessary it was essential to break all ties with the Vatican and to omit any mention of the Pope during services.[195]

In January, 1945, Mgr. Romza tried to reach a *modus vivendi*. But the situation became worse and all the restrictions on religion in the Soviet Union were imposed in Transcarpathia also by the time it was formally incorporated in the Soviet Ukraine on June 28, 1945.[196] In October, Bishop Nestor arrived in Mukachevo, after nomination to the Orthodox See. The Press declared that with his arrival Mgr. Romza's jurisdiction had ceased and his Catholic diocese should pass to the Orthodox bishop. The events in Galicia also began to have their repercussions. Several times Mgr. Romza was questioned by the NKVD, instructed in the 'misdeeds' of the Church, the Pope and the hierarchy and invited to become Orthodox. He always replied: 'Suffering and death are preferable to betraying the Church'.[197]

The crisis came in 1947. At Easter, following the deportation of two Basilian Fathers for their refusal to become Orthodox, Mgr. Romza preached two stirring sermons. As the feast of the Assumption approached, the occasion of great pilgrimages to Mukachevo, he was forbidden to go to the town. The appearance of some 80,000 Catholics for the feast apparently convinced the Communists that the diocese could be liquidated only by force.[198] On October 27 the carriage in which Mgr. Romza was returning from consecrating a church was rammed by a truck loaded with police and soldiers. The Bishop, who escaped unhurt, was then attacked with iron bars; he died in the hospital of Mukachevo.[199]

Anti-Vatican propaganda continued and early in 1952 this was given added impetus by further charges against the Vatican of organising murder within the USSR. In October, 1949, the Ukrainian writer, Yaroslav Galan, was killed in Lvov by 'nationalist murderers', according to an original account.[200] His post-war literary activities had been notable for a number of pamphlets which 'unmasked . . . the reactionary nature of the Vatican, the centre of Catholic reaction.'[201] Little was made of the affair at the time but in March, 1952, his memory was revived by the posthumous award of a Second Class Stalin Prize for his pamphlets.[202] Designed to show that 'the history of the Vatican is a long chain of treachery, corruption, blood, blackmail, political intrigue and vile ravaging of the human soul', these included *The Father of Darkness and His Associates, Blood and Chains* and *The Twilight of Alien Gods*, recounting 'the tragic history of the forced union with Papal Rome imposed on the people of Transcarpathia over 350 years ago'.[203] Responsibility for Galan's death was now laid at the

Pope's door. Konstantin Simonov, Deputy General Secretary of the Soviet Writers' Union, declared: 'The writer Yaroslav Galan fell at his post, he perished at the hands of murderers sent from the Vatican'.[204] *Izvestiya* asserted :'The writer fell a victim to the revenge of Catholic murders'.[205]

Since 1954 Soviet Catholics have had a history largely similar to that of other religious organisations in the USSR. In 1955, during the relative lull which followed the November, 1954, Decree, sanction was given for the consecration in Lithuania of two new Catholic bishops, Julionas Stepanovicius and Petras Mazelis,* and Christmas congregations there were said to have included 'many priests who have returned from exile this year'.[206]

The anti-Catholic propaganda, which has been put out since the intensification of the anti-religious campaign in 1957–58, has likewise included not only outward-looking and pseudo-academic works such as M. M. Sheinman's *The Papacy* (1959) and I. Lavretsky's *The Cardinals are Going to Hell* † (1962) but also a wealth of material vilifying the local Catholic clergy. In October, 1959, for example, in the course of a description of the scandalous life of monks at the Catholic monastery of the Holy Spirit in Lithuania, a priest Evstafi was stated to have kept a diary of his many seductions and the Father Superior Antonii and the deacon Veniamin were denounced for homosexuality.[207] In March, 1964, a Catholic apostate in Latvia publicly denounced his former fellow-priests for alleged careerism and avarice.[208] Similar charges had previously been made by another apostate priest, I. Ragauskas. A fourth edition of his book *Ite Missa Est* was published in Lithuanian in 1963, shortly after a Latvian language edition had appeared.[209]

Catholics, too, have been selected as targets for 'individual work'. In November, 1960, the journal *Nauka i Religiya* cited a case from Byelorussia:

'There is a Catholic church in Kobrin. The priest had begun a long time ago to keep his eye on Richard Oglensky. He took his

* Bishop Mazelis's death was announced by *Tass* (in English) on May 25, 1966.

† The first of these works was put out by the USSR Academy of Sciences, and associated Pope John XXIII with the aim of uniting 'the bourgeois world in a kind of spiritual NATO'; I. Lavretsky's book set out to demonstrate the reactionary character of 'St. Peter's sinking ship'.

mother on as a church cleaner and began to try to bring the young man to be one of his acolytes and taught him how to play the organ and designed a great future for him. Richard works as a postman and at the same time is studying at a school of working youth. The Catholic priest realised that it would be useful to maintain contacts with believers through a postman.

'When Richard began serving in the Catholic Church, the atheists B. M. Berlin, V. N. Vladimirov and others, after finding out about this, took him under their wing. They talked with him patiently and gave him books to read. At first Richard visited the church as previously. However, the work with him did not cease until the atheists had gained their objective. The young man ceased to believe in God.'[210]

In June, 1963, an article in *Nauka i Religiya* deploring counter-productive excesses revealed that in the Lithuanian town of Anikschyai a common practice of propagandists was to go up to local Catholics and warn them: 'Don't you dare, so-and-so, to go to church or else. . . .' This was largely ineffective as Catholics would then go off to mass and confession at the nearby towns of Troshkunai or Kovarskas. In the same town a 14- or 15-year-old boy would often be seen outside the church taking down the names of people who entered. He had been told at school to 'expose' those pupils who went to church.[211]

Lithuania has also seen determined efforts to substitute secular for religious ceremonial. Of the ten new festivals established by the end of 1961 the Winter Festival was designed to fall shortly before Shrovetide, the Spring Festival a week before Easter and Sowing Festivals were celebrated in many areas on local Patron Saints' Days.[212] Steps have also been taken to obstruct religious festivals and observances. In June, 1962, when many pilgrims were on their way to the Vilnius Calvary, traffic inspectors stationed on the route stopped all cars with passengers and told them bluntly: 'There is no reason for you to go on a pilgrimage.'[213]

A more recent example of direct action was the sending of a commission of experts into the vaults of the Dominican church in Vilnius to expose the 'miracle' of the many mummified bodies which have lain there for centuries. In May, 1964, it was announced that the vaults were to be opened to the public so that it 'can be convinced yet again to what methods the obscurantists resort in order to work on the feelings of believers'.[214]

There have also been reports of the closing of Catholic churches—in August, 1962, 20 were said to have been closed in the Grodno region of Byelorussia[215]—and trials of Catholic priests. In September, 1959, a priest in Latvia was sentenced to a year's 'corrective labour' for organising religious instruction for young people,[216] and in the following November a village priest in Lithuania was sentenced to nine months' 'corrective labour' for having instructed 30 children in 'the law of God'.[217] Considerable propaganda was made out of the trial in June, 1962, of two Lithuanian Catholic priests, who were sentenced to eight and four years' imprisonment respectively for 'criminal currency operations and speculation' connected with the building of a new church in Klaipeda. This propaganda began the day before the trial with the publication in *Pravda* of an attack on the defendants under the title of 'Scoundrels in Black Cassocks'.[218]

Meanwhile parish priests and congregations in many localities continued actively to resist attempts at encroachment by local party or specialised atheist organisations. In August, 1962, *Komsomolskaya Pravda* told the story of a girl—Mariya Zverzhevich—who lived in Odelsk in the Grodno region of Byelorussia, where 'the well-trained Catholic priest, Peter Bortashevich, had for years used all available means to keep the inhabitants of the village in the Catholic web'. Mariya's grandmother was said to have beaten her when she joined the Pioneers, and again when she secretly took part in Pioneer meetings, so Mariya had run off to live with her class teacher and the director of her school. In 1961, on the day after she had openly paraded for the first time in her red Pioneer scarf in Odelsk, her class teacher sent her to a boarding school in Grodno. On the way 'hysterical religious women' apprehended her in the bus and brought her back to Odelsk, where the Public Prosecutor had to be called to rescue her from their clutches and return her to the boarding school.

The matter had not ended there. Mariya had not liked the boarding school and had been affected by the 'tearful and hypocritical' letters of her grandmother. When relatives appeared at the school, she had returned with them to Odelsk, where she had torn off her Pioneers' scarf and had gone to the Catholic Church to the joy of the 'hysterical religious women' and the Catholic priest.[219]

In November, 1963, the complaint was made that an underground Uniat nunnery in Lvov had been smuggling in crosses and religious literature from abroad.[220]

In 1962 the favourable reaction of the Soviet leadership to Pope John's encyclical *Pacem in Terris* was followed by the granting of permission to representatives of the Russian Orthodox Church to attend the Vatican Council, which was to be reported relatively objectively in the Soviet Press.[221] In February, 1963, Archbishop Slipy, the head of the former Uniat Church in the Ukraine, was released from prison and allowed to go to Rome.[222] In 1963, on the death of Pope John Soviet Press tributes hailed him as 'one of the most important figures in the modern world'.[223]

An article in *Kommunist* in October, 1964, recognised that Communist aims could be furthered by tactical co-operation with 'renovators' like Pope John who had been forced to adopt a 'realistic' approach to certain international issues in order to strengthen the declining influence of religion in the modern world.[224] Further corroboration of this change of attitude appeared in 1965. The main philosophical journal stated in August:

While recognising the profound ideological differences between Marxism and Catholicism, Communists consider that this should not be an obstacle to the joint struggle of atheists and believers in defence of the fundamental interests of the workers.[225]

It was made plain, however, that this development in no way marked a more conciliatory attitude towards Catholics in the Soviet Union. In Lithuania, where the Catholic Church is often denounced as a hotbed of nationalism,[226] it was stated in December, 1963, that:

'The propagandists of atheistic knowledge must never forget that despite certain changes in the views of the ecclesiastical hierarchy on the questions of peace and disarmament, the reactionary nature of religious ideology does not change. We must conduct a decisive struggle against survivals of the past helping believers to recognise the truth, free themselves from their religious fetters and actively join in the building of a new life."[227]

In 1965, the Catholic Church in Lithuania was described as a 'serious opponent, subtle and experienced'. Churchmen propagated nationalistic ideas 'openly hostile to the Socialist system'. A vast network of atheist centres was said to operate throughout Lithuania, its work being planned and co-ordinated by a Republican Council. In places where Party organisations neglected the materialist education of workers, 'clergymen and

[96]

sectarians built their nests and the influence of the Communist Party was weakened'.[228]

In October, 1966, a Museum of Atheism, opened in Vilnius, was said to rank second in the Soviet Union. The only other similar sized atheist museum was that in Leningrad.[229]

In the absence of any comprehensive statistics from Soviet sources the only available estimate of the state of the Catholic Church in the Soviet Union is that given in the 1966 edition of the official Vatican Year Book. This lists the following information:[230]

LATVIA

Archdiocese of Riga:

> Churches 116, diocesan priests 120, priests consecrated in previous year 1, seminarists 28, religious houses 4 with 47 inmates,* Catholics 476,963.*

Suffragan Diocese of Liepaya:

> Churches 50.* Catholics 89,617.

LITHUANIA

Archdiocese of Kaunas:

> Churches 240, diocesan priests 277, priests consecrated in previous year 11, seminarists 48, religious houses 43 with 420 inmates,* Catholics 560,000.*

Suffragan Diocese of Kaisedorys:

> Churches 104, diocesan priests 102, priests consecrated in previous year 0, seminarists 5, religious houses 10 with 65 inmates,* Catholics 224,700.

Suffragan Diocese of Panevezys:

> Churches 207, diocesan priests 245, priests consecrated in previous year 5, seminarists 6, religious houses 12 with 102 inmates,* Catholics 418,950.

Suffragan Diocese of Telsiai:

> Churches 143, diocesan priests 268, priests consecrated in previous year 4, seminarists 32, religious houses 12 with 97 inmates,* Catholics 385,872.*

Suffragan Diocese of Vilkaviskis:

> Churches 120, diocesan priests 214, priests consecrated in previous year 5, seminarists 33, religious houses 18 with 117 inmates,* Catholics 350,000.*

Archdiocese of Vilna (Vilnius):

Number of churches not given, diocesan priests 243, priests consecrated in previous year 4, seminarists 28, religious houses 26 with 211 inmates, Catholics 279,832.

BYELORUSSIA

Diocese of Pinsk:

Number of churches not given, diocesan priests 88, priests consecrated in previous year 2, seminarists 14, religious houses (women only) 8 with 54 inmates, Catholics 92,000.

But these figure are likely to be considerably inflated. Those marked with an asterisk are identical with those published in the 1945 edition of the Vatican Year Book. The information given for the Archdiocese of Vilnius in 1966 may be compared with that published in the Year Book's 1964 edition. In the latter, the number of Catholics, for example, was given as 1,485,484—the figure given in 1945. The figures for seminarists are also likely to be unduly high. An émigré source reported that in 1963 the Kaunas seminary was allowed to accept only five new entrants.[231] According to later reports, this seminary is the only one left open.[232] The only yardsticks for comparing the other statistics are isolated figures given in Soviet broadcasts to foreign audiences. In recent years these have given the number of functioning Catholic churches as 1,235,[233] the number of priests as 1,270[234] and the number of Catholics in the Soviet Union as about 4,000,000.[235]

(c) PROTESTANTISM

Russian Protestantism was a protest against Tsarist State intervention in the affairs of the Russian Orthodox Church; it was also a protest against the secularisation of that Church and its support of social injustice. Broadly speaking, it stood for democratic ideals and a free Church in a free State.[236] The numerous sects were never more than semi-legal and were often officially persecuted.[237] The most important ones at the beginning of the 20th century were the Evangelical Christians and the Baptists. Though both adhered to essentially Baptist principles they interpreted them differently. For the Union of Evangelical Christians, founded in 1908, represented an already Russified Protestantism, whereas Baptism had been imported from Germany in the 1870s and the Russian Baptist Union, founded in 1884, closely followed the foreign Baptists. In 1914 there were not more than 8,472 Evangelical Christians, though they were rapidly increasing, while the Baptist Union numbered 97,000 baptised members. Difficult years followed for both sects because of their fervent pacifism. Many followers were persecuted and large numbers of their chapels and meeting-houses closed.[238] By 1916 the number of Baptists was reduced to 60,000.[239]

The Russian Bolsheviks recognised early the democratic influence of the sects and sought to make use of them. In the summer of 1903 the Second Congress of the Russian Social Democratic Workers' Party resolved:

'Taking into account that the sectarian movement in Russia is in many of its manifestations one of the democratic currents directed against the existing order of things the Second Congress directs the attention of all Party members to work among sectarians for the purpose of attracting them to Social-Democracy.'[240]

After the Revolution the sectarians gained more than they lost by the decree of January 23, 1918, separating the Church from the State. Baptism spread rapidly in European Russia and Siberia, while the Evangelical Christians were, for a time, openly favoured by the Government, in order to weaken the Orthodox Church; the official printers actually published 175,000 books and pamphlets for Evangelical propaganda. By 1922 the membership of the Evangelical Christian Union exceeded 250,000.[241] Efforts were made to fuse with the All-Russian Baptist Union and in 1921 an agreement for amalgamation was signed. But, beyond the nomination of joint Relief and School Committees, it came to nothing.[242]

The Communists went to remarkable lengths in tolerating the sects at this time. The decree of January 4, 1919,[243] permitting religious conscientious objectors to serve in hospitals—preferably those for contagious diseases—instead of in the Red Army, was enacted largely for their benefit. An attitude of positive benevolence was adopted towards the sectarian communities working small farms collectively. An early decree of the Commissariat of Justice declared:

'These sects adapt themselves quite readily to the common civil Soviet laws and regulations and organically unite as agricultural

[99]

nuclei into Soviet organisations, in spite of the religious form which their Communist tendencies, as a result of historical conditions, have adopted. The task of Soviet organs in regard to these organisations consists pre-eminently in seeing these Communist organisations, developed and fortified with the aid of science and superior technique, continue in their adopted habits and modes of Communist organisation as industrial-agricultural groups. Raised to a superior form they will serve as practical examples of the possibility and advantage of Communism for the toiling population.'[244]

But the success of the sects soon made the Communists regret their tolerance. The 12th Party Congress in April, 1923, noted with evident alarm 'the considerable growth of certain sects whose leaders are closely connected with well-known elements of the European and American bourgeoisie'. It called for the publication of literature which would 'unmask...the physiognomy and real class nature of the various sects having influence over the popular masses'.[245] Subtlety and extreme care in dealing with the sects were ordered by the 13th Congress the following year:

'A particularly attentive attitude is necessary towards the sectarians, many of whom were subjected to the most cruel persecution on the part of Tsarism and among whom great activity is to be noted. By an intelligent approach it is necessary to direct into the groove of Soviet work the considerable economic-cultural elements among the sectarians. In view of the large numbers of sectarians this work has great significance. The task must be solved in accordance with local conditions.'[246]

The sectarian leaders were no less careful in their behaviour towards the régime, particularly over the question of pacifism. That the Government's granting of exemption was only a temporary concession became clear when the authorities began to complain of 'serious abuses'.[247] and finally arranged court cases at which 'it was established that denial of war does not enter into the dogmas of Baptism and that in bourgeois countries Baptists have frequently taken part in war'.[248] The sectarian leaders gave way. At its 9th Congress in 1923 the Evangelical Christian Union decided to regard military service as an obligation.[249] The 26th Congress of the All-Union Baptist Union in 1927 came out directly in support of conscription for Baptists[250] and openly testified to the 'complete freedom of conscience' granted by the Soviet Government.[251]

Nevertheless the sectarians were doomed once again to persecution. Their successes since 1917 had been too great. By

1928 the Evangelical Christians, for instance, had their own Theological College in Moscow (established December 1, 1927) and 3,219 congregations with at least 4,000,000 members, many of them well-to-do peasants (Kulaks) and Cossacks, small tradesmen and independent artisans,[252] particularly in the Ukraine and Siberia.[253]

The year 1929 opened a decade of almost continuous attacks on the sectarians. The decree of April 8, 1929, imposing severe restrictions on the activities of religious bodies, which is still in force, hit them hard. A number of their organisational centres were closed, including the Theological College.[254] Political trials were staged. Thus in February, 1929, a 25-strong 'band of Baptist spies' was 'discovered' in Minsk. It was alleged that, after attending the Baptist Institute in America, they had 'crossed the frontier and settled in Byelorussia where they carried on espionage'. Another 'band of Baptist spies' was 'discovered' in the Ukraine. Their leader, 'the inveterate spy Shevchuk, founder of one of the Baptist communities in Volhynia', was accused of 'conducting espionage for several years on the orders of the Polish General Staff' and of 'contacting Baptist communities in Volhynia and the Shepetovka, Kiev and Artemovsk regions which he regularly supplied with money from the Polish secret service'.[255]

Collectivisation of agriculture badly affected the sects. Leaders of evangelical prayer meetings and others known to be active in religious life were excluded from membership of the collective farms. The majority were deported, many dying *en route* or in exile.[256] The sectarian farming communities were incorporated into the new collectives despite their objections to farming with unbelievers.[257] They protested in vain that (as the Commissariat of Justice had recognised a decade earlier) they were 'entirely for the Communist programme, for the abolition of the exploitation of man by man, for Socialist property, for the broadest Soviet democracy ... for the full and immediate implementation of Communist principles in agriculture'. Now it was alleged that 'behind the facade of sectarian "communes" kulak elements have tried to defend and preserve typical exploiter enterprises'; but 'the workers' had 'unmasked the hostile face of these "Christian communes"'.[258] By 1939 it was said that 'the sectarian pseudo-communes have been liquidated' and 'in their place real Bolshevik collective farms have been created'.[259]

Propaganda against the sects was bitter and sustained. In 1931 the Evangelical Christian sect was denounced as 'a masked counter-revolutionary kulak organisation receiving financial support from abroad'.[260] Anti-sectarian propaganda became especially violent in the latter 1930s, the years of the Great Purge. Not only were the sectarians accused of 'providing foreign secret services with cadres of spies and informers' but it was implied that their preachers were 'sectarian spies sent into the USSR by the secret services of Western Europe and America'.[261]

By August, 1941, the number of Evangelical Christian communities had been reduced to about 1,000; a hand-out from the Press Department of the Soviet Embassy in London, purporting to record the principal sects surviving in the USSR, did not even mention the Baptists.[262]

But the sects rallied with extraordinary resilience once the official persecution was called off. In June, 1942, the Evangelical Christian and Baptist leaders joined in issuing an appeal to Baptists throughout the world 'in the name of 4,000,000 Russian brothers and sisters'.[263] A similar joint message of sympathy and encouragement was sent in 1943 to 'Evangelical Christians and Baptists under the yoke of the German Fascist invaders'. It exhorted:

'Love your country passionately. Be determined anti-Fascists. Support the partisan movement in your localities.'[264]

Within the Soviet Union the Evangelical Christian and Baptist leaders called on their followers 'to struggle with arms in their hands in the ranks of the Red Army against the Fascists'.[265] In September, 1946, Polyansky, Chairman of the governmental Council for the Affairs of Religious Cults, expressed official satisfaction with the sectarians' war record.[266]

The war brought the Evangelical Christians and Baptists closer together. In October, 1944, they held a joint conference in Moscow, attended by representatives from Moscow, Leningrad, the Ukraine, Byelorussia, the Caucasus, Siberia, the Crimea, the Volga area and Kazakhstan, and agreed on formal unification.[267] In August, 1945, they invited the adhesion of the Pentecostals, a loose association of various sects, all claiming to be guided by the Spirit of God and holding views roughly similar to those of the Quakers but rather different from those of the Baptists.[268] A further conference was held from which emerged the Union of Evangelical Christian-Baptists, uniting over 3,000 communities of many nationalities, including Russians, Ukrainians, Byelorussians, Latvians, Estonians, Lithuanians, Karelo-Finns, Rumanians, Hungarians, Moldavians, Georgians, Armenians and others. An executive organ of eleven, the All-Union Council of Evangelical Christian-Baptists (known as the VSEKhB from its Russian initials), was elected. This Council had a Presidium of six Moscow-resident members, including the Revs. Ya. I. Zhidkov (Evangelical Christian), Chairman; M. I. Golyaev (Baptist), M. I. Orlov (Evangelical Christian), Deputy Chairmen; A. V. Karev (Evangelical Christian), General Secretary. The council also had about 70 plenipotentiaries for republics and senior presbyters for regions (as from April 1, 1947, the plenipotentiaries were renamed senior presbyters,[269]) whose task was to supervise, educate and strengthen the communities and their presbyters and especially to 'implant among believers the glorious cause of unity'.[270] In 1946 the Council began publishing its own periodical, *Bratsky Vestnik.*

Since its inception VSEKhB has been at pains to preserve correct relations with the Soviet authorities, *inter alia* by publicly associating itself with the declared objectives of Soviet foreign policy and by playing its part in the 'peace' campaign. Early Baptist initiatives included an appeal in support of the World Peace Congress in Paris, a protest to the United Nations Security Council against bombing in Korea, a radio appeal to world Baptists and a protest against 'bacteriological warfare' in Korea by Zhidkov.[271] While this has not safeguarded the Baptists from the rigours of the Party's anti-religious campaign, it has helped to preserve an organisational structure, which sees to the regular visiting of Baptist communities in all parts of the Soviet Union. By the end of 1947 there were about 4,000 of these, even though a number of the smaller communities had been amalgamated.[272] Baptised members numbered 400,000, while 4,000,000 attended services.[273] By 1954 the number of communities had increased to 5,400 and the number of Baptised members to 512,000.[274]

Since then the militancy of many rank and file Baptists, as reflected in an extreme case in the attempts of a female worker at a local plywood factory to distribute religious literature and win converts in the Leningrad Museum of the History of Religion and Atheism,[275] coupled with the ability of the Baptists to express their faith in contemporary terms, has led to a further increase in the membership of the Baptist Church. In 1963 *Bratsky Vestnik* stated that 119 new adult members had been received into the Moscow community after serving their two to three years' probation[276] and Soviet sources have complained of considerable Baptist activity in Dzhambul in Kazakhstan, where the community numbers 900[277] and in the Ukraine town of Dneprodzerzhinsk where the Baptists were credited with gaining 30 converts between 1962 and 1963.[278]

This activity has inevitably made the Baptists an important target of the intensified anti-religious campaign. Since 1957–58 anti-Baptist propaganda has not only made much of the contention that 'many Baptists are used as American spies'[279] and sought to discredit Baptists through statements by apostates testifying to their essential 'hypocrisy'. It has also made determined efforts to refute Baptist teaching, particularly the compatibility between scientific achievements and religious experience. Early in 1961, for example, *Nauka i Religiya* devoted articles in successive issues to debunking a Baptist typewritten pamphlet, which purported to be a stenographic report of a debate in Tallin, during which a local Baptist factory-hand had routed the leading atheists, including an astronomer, a doctor and a philosopher. This pamphlet, it was stated, had been circulating widely in Kuibyshev.[280]

To judge from Press reports, Baptists in many areas have been specially singled out for 'individual work', but this has been far from universally successful. In 1961, for example, Losnikov, the 23-year-old son of the Baptist choir-master in Frunze, refused to recant so as to regain admittance to a local technical college, after a five-hour meeting with his fellow-workers had 'turned into an out-an-out atheistic platform'. (He had previously resigned after being worked on by atheist activists.[281]) More recently, Stepanov, a brigade leader at a repair and construction administration in Riga, refused even to express regret when being taxed at a workers' meeting with having distributed protests alleging that believers were persecuted in the Soviet Union and with having tried to send this 'slander' abroad.[282]

And it is probably this 'obstinacy' which has led to the summary treatment which Baptists have received in many areas. In Dneprodzerzhinsk, for example, an engineer at the State District Power Station, whose high standard of work entitled him to 80 roubles a month, was paid at the lower rate of 70 roubles and told bluntly 'leave the sect and you will get more pay'.[283] In Kshen in the Kursk Region, after the head doctor at the local hospital had failed to secure the recantation of an active Baptist epidemiologist, the Deputy Chairman of the Executive Committee of the District Soviet went in person to see him at his apartment and took a militiaman with him. What became of the Baptist epidemiologist was not then revealed, but the fact it was stated that he had since become 'a martyr in the eyes of believers', suggested that the consequences were drastic.[284] Similarly a driving instructor at a centre in Melitopol was told by his director that:

'In the District Party Committee they are calling me the director of the Baptist centre because of you. . . . So let us decide. . . . Will you renounce your religion? No? . . . Well then, send me in your resignation.'[285]

Official criticism of these measures has essentially stemmed from their failure to achieve their objective. In contrast, when in 1962 in the Tula region, after 'atheists had toured the homes of believers for individual work', two girl Baptists went on hunger strike 'until the persecution of us by the atheists ceases', *Izvestiya* denounced this as blackmail and demanded that the local Baptist leader 'be sentenced with all the severity of our laws'.[286]

At the same time severe measures have been taken against those Baptists who, not recognising the authority of the VSEKhB, have organised illegal (*i.e.*, unregistered) communities, and have engaged in active propaganda of their faith. In 1962 one Baptist preacher, A. F. Prokofiev, was sentenced to five years' imprisonment to be followed by five years' exile. He was stated to have toured towns in the RSFSR, the Ukraine, Byelorussia and Kazakhstan, and to have visited Tashkent conducting 'seething underground missionary activities'. He had distributed 'sermons, epistles and letters containing malicious slander against Soviet reality', and had even tried, while in Kharkov, to dispatch them 'illegally across the frontier'.[287]

Prokofiev's name was mentioned again in 1964 when three leaders of an illegal Baptist community in Tashkent were tried and sentenced. On Prokofiev's instructions they were said to have set up 'a so-called initiative group' in Tashkent, to have 'slandered Soviet reality' and to have demanded 'freedom of religious propaganda'. They had not only 'copied, roneoed and distributed provocative literature (local and foreign)... and protests among believers' but had 'organised individual or group listening to special sermons transmitted in Russian by radio stations in the USA, Canada and Ecuador, put them on tape and later propagated these in every way they could'.[288]

Earlier it had been revealed that a woman in Leningrad, L. V. Mikryukova, who had in 1963 lost custody of six of her children to Robert Malozemov, her son by a previous marriage, had also been an assistant of Prokofiev's.[289] This may well have weighed with the People's Court, which agreed with the Komsomol Malozemov's plea that 'it is necessary to wrest them from the black nets of the Baptists and to bring them up as real Soviet people'.[290]

Prokofiev was also stated to have been the original inspiration behind a militant unregistered community in Kotsovskoe in Moldavia. This community had been distributing 'anti-Soviet leaflets' protesting against the alleged 'repressions to which believers are subjected'. It had even composed a letter to the Soviet Government on this subject. Among its members was the previously mentioned epidemiologist who had evidently been forced to leave Kshen as a result of the measures taken against him.[291]

In 1965 it became known that Prokofiev and G. Yu. Kryuchkov had a few years before formed a group to convene an All-Union Congress of EKhB to replace the existing church leadership, which the group accused of betraying the true faith and acting contrary to God's word.[292] In 1966, Prokofiev, described as 'a dangerous State criminal', was said to be serving his third jail sentence.[293]

Other trials of leaders of illegal Baptist communities were reported from the Byelorussian town of Brest, from Namangan in Uzbekistan and from Kulunda in the Altai. The trial of four leaders of the community in Brest began on May 13, 1963, after an article in *Pravda* the previous January had pointed to the community's illegal activities, which, it stated, were being organised by Stepan Matviyuk, a one-time deserter from the Soviet Army and a former associate of Bandera, the Ukrainian nationalist leader[294] (killed by a Soviet agent in Munich in 1961). This community was stated to have been established when 200 of the 300 Baptists in Brest had refused to link up with a nearby registered community and subordinate themselves to the VSEKhB. While taking every precaution against exposure by constant switching of prayer meetings from one suburb of Brest to another, the community was said to have 'actively reproduced and disseminated the "calls", appeals and "protests" of their "organising committees" not only among themselves' and to have also 'made missionary journeys to their "brothers and sisters in Christ" in the Kamenets and Kobrin districts, the town of Pinsk and even the Orenburg region'. In addition they listened to broadcasts from foreign Baptist centres, recorded extracts and relayed them to their fellow Baptists.[295] No details of the sentences were published, but they are likely to have been heavy. In the trial at Namangan, reported in November, 1963, three leaders of an illegal community were given two-year prison sentences on the comparatively minor charge of actively engaging in religious propaganda.[296]

In the case of the Kulunda community, its origin was traced back to 1961 when the younger Baptists in the area came out in open criticism of the VSEKhB and formed their own unregistered community. They had since attracted adolescents into their sect, and had called on their members not to carry out civil duties, or to take part in trade union work or to obey the volunteer police (the *druzhinniki*).* They had also held illegal prayer meetings at three or four in the morning and had set up 'an illegal school for the instruction of young Baptists'. Their leader was given five years' imprisonment and two of his assistants three years.[299]

The existence of these unregistered communities was an important issue at an All-Union Congress of Evangelical Christian-Baptists in Moscow from October 15 to October 17, 1963. The Congress not only furnished details of an 'initiative group' which had been operating in the Ukraine, and with particular success in the Donetsk, Kharkov and Lugansk areas,[300] but directly declared:

'We warn all our brothers and sisters against various kinds of

* Similar charges as well as their refusal to allow their members to undertake military service or participate in elections have formed the basis for many recent trials of members of the outlawed sects, the Pentecostals (or Shakers) and Jehovah's Witnesses. Pentecostal communities are known to have existed in Kalinin, Donetsk, Ussuriisk, Ryazan and Saratov,[297] while groups of Jehovah's Witnesses have been found in the Ukraine, Moldavia, Chuvashia, Tataria, the Kurgan and Tomsk regions and Kazakhstan.[298]

missives which contain dangerous attempts and attempts damaging to all the work of the Lord in our country which are aimed at creating strained relations between our brotherhood and the authorities and rulers in our country.'[301]

The Congress, which approved the 1962 application of the VSEKhB to join the World Council of Churches and its acceptance in February, 1963,[302] also revealed that the VSEKhB had in 1956 published 15,000 hymnals and in 1957 had issued an edition of the Bible of 10,000 copies. At the same time it was stated that 'there has since been no opportunity of issuing new editions of the Bible and of Collections of Spiritual Songs'.[303] On October 21 the VSEKhB elected a new Presidium: Ya. I. Zhidkov (Chairman), N. A. Levindanto and A. L. Anreev (Deputy Chairmen), A. V. Karev (General Secretary) and I. G. Ivanov (Treasurer).[304]

But the Congress gave no figures for the number of Soviet Baptists. Outside sources have estimated this at 1,500,000 full members with a total community of 3,000,000. These figures, while they probably take account of unregistered communities, are almost certainly too high. The VSEKhB gave a figure of 545,000 full members when it applied for membership of the World Council of Churches in 1962.[305] This contrasts with a Soviet figure of only 'about 2,000 registered communities' with 'more than 200,000' members, given in 1965.[306]

The warning issued to dissident Baptists at the 1963 Congress has evidently gone unheeded and the rift in the Baptist Church has widened. Resistance to Soviet and VSEKhB authority, which closely parallels reported discontent within the Orthodox Church,* has been widespread and well-organised. Under the leadership of their 'organising committee' headed by Kryuchkov and George Vins, representatives of the 'schismatics' or 'Prokofievans' petitioned government officials at all levels, demanding an All-Union Baptist Congress and an end to the 'interference of school and State in the upbringing of believers' children'.[307] According to *Nauka i Religiya* in July, 1966, 'large groups of believers' were summoned to Moscow to enforce their demands. On a recent occasion this had led to a 'gross violation of public order outside a government building' and administrative organs had been forced to take 'retaliatory measures'.[308] In 1966 the dissident Baptists stepped

* See page 62.

up their 'propaganda of resistance to Soviet laws'. The *orgkomitet* set forth its demands for complete religious freedom in widely-circulated underground literature, including its bulletin, the *Bratski Listok*.[309] The *orgkomitet* was said to have won support by exploiting 'mistakes' made by local authorities in dealing with believers.[310]

The Soviet authorities are evidently concerned about the growing influence of the Baptists, particularly their success in weaning young people away from Communist influence. In August, 1966, six dissident Baptist leaders in Rostov-on-Don were imprisoned for persistent infringement of the law on the separation of Church from State and School from Church.[311] Charges against them included organising a street procession and public baptism of about 40 young people, thereby causing a disturbance, circulating anti-Soviet literature and running illegal Sunday schools, all of which were defined as offences against this legislation in a resolution passed by the RSFSR Supreme Soviet in March.* In February, a *Pravda* article, signed by two factory workers, had described the illegal activities of the Rostov Baptists, and demanded that violators of this law should no longer go unpunished.[312] In October five more dissident Baptists were reported to have been jailed in Kiev for two to three years for similar offences against the revised legislation.[313] Other trials of Baptists in 1966 included that of two women in Kirgizia, who received five-year sentences in March for running Sunday schools and inciting young people to refrain from joining the Pioneer and Komsomol organisations.[314]†

In August, however, the Chairman of the Council for Religious Affairs emphasised the need to distinguish the movement's recalcitrant leaders from their followers, most of whom were said to be honest citizens 'led into criminal activity' through ignorance of Soviet law.[315] The effect of indiscriminate anti-Baptist propaganda on some sections of the community had been illustrated by incidents in Mtsensk in the

---

* See page 63.

† Under Article 227 of the RSFSR Criminal Code, which is open to wide interpretation, the organisation of a group which, under the guise of performing religious rites, conducts activities which 'cause harm to citizens' health' or 'induce citizens to refrain from social activity', and the drawing of minors into such a group, are punishable by up to five years' deprivation of liberty.

Orel region, described in *Izvestiya* in June. After the murder of a three-year-old boy by a dissident Baptist woman, special militia units were needed to protect the family concerned from the 'elemental wrath' of the townspeople, and cries of 'get the Baptists' and 'the Baptists are slaughtering our children' were heard all over the town. *Izvestiya* pointed out that, although the deranged mind of the murderess had been influenced by sectarian teaching, ritual killing was 'alien to the faith and convictions of the Baptists'.[316] Nevertheless in July *Selskaya Zhizn* published a letter by an anonymous reader describing how she had been persuaded by sectarian 'brothers and sisters' to murder her illegitimate child by throwing it under a train and had been foiled in her attempt only at the last minute.[317]

The Lutherans and Seventh-Day Adventists are the most important of the other Protestant Churches in the Soviet Union, all of which have been exposed to similar pressures.° Before the Revolution the Lutherans, who were mainly Germans, Estonians and Latvians, had churches in practically every large town in European Russia. However, they were to suffer greatly during the forced collectivisation of agriculture, when they were accused of 'dozens of cases of provocation and savage murder, as well as arson of barns, haylofts and cattlesheds'[321] and by the summer of 1936 the number of pastors still in office had been reduced to ten.[322] Terror against Lutherans flared up again in 1937 during Stalin's purges and by the end of that year there were no Lutheran pastors still in office and no Lutheran parish existed anywhere in the Soviet Union. In 1940, however, the annexation of Estonia and Latvia once again made the Lutheran Church an effective religious organisation in the USSR. In 1961 the Latvian Lutheran Church was stated to have 270 churches[323] and it is estimated to have some 500,000 to 600,000 members.[324] The Estonian Evangelical Lutheran Church is thought to have a total congregation of 350,000.[325]

It is not known for certain over how many members the All-Union Council of Seventh-Day Adventists, which publishes its own journal *Valgus*,[326] exercises jurisdiction. In 1954 the

---

° There have been accounts of 'painstaking individual work' among members of these communities,[318] their religious leaders have been vilified—one Lutheran pastor was denounced for allegedly plying adolescents with cigarettes and vodka and instructing them in depravity[319]—and Adventist leaders have been tried and given severe sentences.[320]

General Conference of Sevent-Day Adventists in Washington estimated that there were 40,000 Adventists in the USSR[327]. A Soviet source gave the number of Adventists in 1964 as 21,500, compared with 12,500 in 1947.[328] It is known, however, that Adventists communities exist in Moscow, the Ukraine, the Baltic area, Moldavia, Tomsk, Rostov, Novossibirsk and some other areas.[329] In 1963 a tribute was paid to their activeness in Latvia, when their practice of having a deacon to visit every 10–15 people and report on their 'spiritual condition' and attendance at services was pointed to as being worthy of emulation by local atheist organisations.[330]

Other Protestant sects include the Mennonites and Molokans. The Mennonites originated in Germany in the 16th century and Mennonite emigration to Russia began two centuries later. In 1924 the Mennonite leaders issued a memorandum to the USSR Central Executive Committee demanding exemption from military service, the right to teach their faith in schools and the right to organise special activities for children. When these demands were rejected many left the Soviet Union.[331] In 1956 there were about 125 Mennonite villages with a total population of 15,000 to 20,000 scattered over Siberia, the Altai and Kazakhstan.[332] Soviet sources now stress the alien origin of the Mennonites and their ties with West Germany. A Mennonite leader in Alma-Ata, the capital of Kazakhstan, was said to have written down all the members of his family as citizens of West Germany at the time of the 1959 Census.[333] In October, 1963, a number of Mennonites were present at the All-Union Congress of Evangelical Christian-Baptists,[334] which looked forward, as an ultimate aim, to drawing all Mennonites into the VSEKhB.[335]

The Molokans trace their origins back to the 18th century. Their name is derived from the Russian word *moloko* (milk) and was originally a nickname they received from their practice of drinking milk during Lent, which was forbidden by the Orthodox Church. They are now most active in Azerbaidzhan. In 1958 it was stated that in the large Molokan community of Khilmili, 60 miles from Baku, there had not been a single marriage at which a Molokan presbyter had not been present.[336] Elsewhere they have fared worse. In 1962 it was claimed that in villages in the Tambov area, where there had been about 4,000 Molokans in 1915, there were then less than a hundred.[337] According to a Soviet authority, however, there has been no noticeable decline in the number of Molokans during the last ten to 15 years. In Georgia, where there are said to be 3,300 registered Molokans, not a single Molokan had renounced his faith in the last 20 years.[338]

(d) JUDAISM

Under the Tsars Judaism was accorded only the lowest degree of official recognition. Hebrews were almost completely debarred from administrative posts, restricted in the choice of professional careers and forbidden to live outside the 'Pale of Settlement', *i.e.*, some of Russia's western provinces.[339] The grounds for this discrimination were religious.

In 1913 Stalin indicated the Bolsheviks' attitude clearly enough when he spoke contemptuously of the 'petrified religious rites and fading psychological relics' of the Jews.[340]

After the October Revolution Judaism was subjected to the general restrictions imposed by the Soviet régime on all religious organisations and a particularly determined campaign was waged to discredit observance of the Sabbath and such Jewish festivals as the Passover, the *Rosh ha-Shanah* (the Jewish New Year) and the *Yom Kippur* (Day of Atonement).[341]

In the early 1930s pressure against the Jewish faith intensified with the denunciation of rabbis for 'instigating bourgeois nationalism'.[342] The decree of 1918 on the separation of Church and State was now interpreted so strictly that the training of rabbis had to be carried on illegally. In 1930 the synagogues in Minsk, for instance, were attacked for operating clandestine religious schools.[343]

Towards the end of the decade the situation deteriorated. The 'triumph of Socialism' was said to have 'evoked among the Hebrew clergy a new access of malice against the Communist Party and Soviet régime'. Practising Jews were accused of 'making every effort to develop religious propaganda among the masses as widely as possible, to preserve untouched the remnants of the old religious way of life, to distort the exact and clear sense of the provisions of the Stalin Constitution on questions of religion, to get their henchmen into the Soviets'.[344]

In the same period a 'hostile nest of rabbis' was 'discovered' by the NKVD in the Choral (Central) Synagogue in Moscow. 'Hiding behind the mask of religion' they had allegedly executed 'tasks for the Fascist secret services', mainly by sending

'agents for the disruption of Socialist construction' in Birobid-
zhan. They were also charged with maintaining 'underground'
religious schools, 'into which the sons of rabbis, former mer-
chants, counter-revolutionary émigrés were recruited'.[345] The
clandestine centres of religious instruction, which had continued to exist, were exposed and denounced to the police by
Der Emes and other officially sponsored Yiddish-language
papers.[346] The same fate befell the prayer meetings organised in
private houses to escape police control. These were denounced
as centres of 'anti-Soviet work'.[347]

By the outbreak of war, in 1941, there were in all 1,011 synagogues and 2,559 rabbis in the USSR as compared with the
1,003 registered Hebrew communities which had existed in the
Ukraine alone in 1926.[348]

Jewish support for the national war effort was voiced by
Rabbi Chobrutsky, President of the Moscow Jewish Community, who greeted Stalin in November, 1942:

'In the name of practising Jews . . . we send up warm prayers to
the Almighty that he may grant you, beloved leader, chosen of
God . . . unbounded wisdom and strength for the speedy and complete annihilation of the cannibal Hitler. . . . We practising Jews are
thoroughly convinced that his victory will be granted by God to
our heroic Red Army which proceeds from victory to victory under
your great, direct and wise guidance and under the glorious banner
of the Great October.'[349]

Their support did not, however, win the Jews the right to
establish any form of central organisation to administer the
various scattered Jewish communities, and this still remains
one of the anomalies between the official status accorded to
Judaism and that accorded to several other recognised faiths
in the USSR.

After the war Stalin's anti-Jewish campaign of the late 1940s
and early 1950s had a paralysing effect on Jewish religious
life. Although it was formally directed against assimilated and
largely atheist Jewish 'bourgeois nationalists' and 'homeless
cosmopolitans', its effect was to discourage the display of any
special Jewishness, of which visiting a synagogue was an obvious manifestation.

In contrast, since 1954 the Jewish faith has in the main been
subjected to the same varying pressures as have other religious
organisations in the Soviet Union. In the comparative lull in
1954–1957, for example, while public statements by Jewish

leaders were being quoted in support of the World Peace Council and against atomic war[350] and the Anglo-French-Israeli action in Egypt,[351] Moscow's Jews were allowed to publish a prayer book (the Peace Prayer-book or *Molitvennik Mir*)[352] and to open a *Yeshiva**** for training rabbis.[353]

In the intensified propaganda which began to be directed against Judaism, determined efforts were made to discredit both Jewish practices and Jewish leaders. Attacks were made on 'the venomous prayers' in the Peace Prayer-book[355] and wide publicity was given to alleged brawling at many synagogues including those at Frunze[356] and Leningrad.[357] Rabbis were also lampooned for their alleged mercenariness. In 1961 a review of the Soviet 'documentary' 'The Road from Darkness' described how:

'For these "saints" nothing is holy. Though in fact there is just one thing they consider holy: money, money and money. And it flows into the pockets of religious parasites. Take the Jewish synagogue in Alma-Ata. The cinema camera has caught its functionaries engaged in "holy" work. The baking of matzot is going on feverishly. They have to hurry; tens of thousands of roubles worth of this product is to be sold within the space of a few days. These pious people have arranged the "export" of matzot to Frunze too, providing, moreover, their own cars for the purpose.'[358]

In the same year the denunciation of the synagogue at Lvov as a centre for speculation in gold, precious stones and foreign currency and the subsequent dispatch of members of its *dvadtsatka* (lay council of 20 members) to corrective labour colonies was used as a pretext for demanding the closure of this synagogue.[359] This demand was met in 1962.[360]

In recent years a large number of synagogues have been closed. An illustration of how these have been effected was given in 1961 in a Moldavian Party journal, which declared of one locality:

'The synagogue also ceased its activity. Its premises were turned into a sports hall. This was preceded by large scale explanatory work among the believers. We began with the leadership—the "twenty elders". After members of this group had been persuaded that the further existence of the congregation was inexpedient, we

* In 1962 it was reported that of the 15 students studying there the previous year nine, who hailed from Georgia, had been refused the necessary residence permits to continue their studies in Moscow.[354]

[114]

used some of them for convincing the remaining believers. All members of the congregation were then divided into groups and each group was taken care of by agitators. As soon as the members of the "council of twenty" signed a statement of resignation, it was comparatively easy to convince the rank and file members of the congregation.'[361]

At the same time the party-sponsored campaign against Judaism has had a number of distinctive features. These include attempts to cast suspicion on a number of synagogues and to insulate them from contacts with foreigners by periodically denouncing the activities of Israeli diplomats and describing religious Jews as 'Israeli agents'.[362] In 1961 two members of the Leningrad synagogue were each sentenced to seven years' imprisonment and a third member to four years for maintaining 'criminal contacts with certain members of an Embassy of one of the capitalist States accredited in Moscow' and for giving them 'information which has been used abroad to the detriment of the Soviet State'.[363]

Another peculiar feature has been the openly anti-semitic cartoons which have sometimes accompanied propaganda against Judaism.[364] In 1964 the appearance abroad of copies of T. K. Kichko's *Judaism Without Embellishment*, put out the previous year by the Ukrainian Academy of Sciences, raised a storm of protest. The book was denounced in the British,[365] French[366] and Italian[367] Communist Press. Following this unprecedented criticism from Communist Parties abroad the Ideological Commission attached to the CPSU Central Committee condemned the work on the grounds that 'a number of erroneous statements contained in the brochure and the illustrations may offend the feelings of believers and may be interpreted in the spirit of anti-semitism'.[368]

At the local level this 'spirit of anti-semitism' was maintained in the burning of synagogues at Malakhovka, a suburb of Moscow, in October, 1959, and in the small town of Tskhakaya in Georgia, in May, 1962,[369] as well as in the persistence of so-called 'blood libels'. These maintain that orthodox Jews need Christian blood for making matzot or unleavened bread for the Passover. In 1962, a Jewish chemist, N. N. Bomze, in the Georgian town of Tskhaltubo, was charged with drawing blood from the face and neck of a Georgian boy and with selling it to the synagogue in the nearby town of Kutaisi. Bomze was severely interrogated and transferred to the Kutaisi jail. He was eventually released at the intervention of the Georgian Chief Prosecutor, who quashed the proceedings, but Bomze was ordered out of the Republic 'for his own safety'.[370]

In contrast with these local aberrations the restrictions placed on the baking of matzot could only be construed as an act of deliberate policy. Before 1957, matzot was regularly supplied by State bakeries. But in that year the practice ceased in Kharkov and by 1961 the ban had been extended to all areas of the Soviet Union except Moscow, Leningrad, Transcaucasia and Central Asia. In 1962 the ban became total[371] and, while individuals were not prevented from baking matzot, the sale of it made those involved liable to prosecution for speculation. In January, 1963, a Moscow trial of a number of Jews for just this offence ended with prison sentences on three of the accused.[372]

Following strong criticism of these restrictions abroad it was disclosed that Moscow's Jewish community had been allowed to rent a bakery for preparing matzot for the 1964 Passover.[373] However, the special dispensation issued by the Chief Rabbi of Moscow permitting those who could not obtain matzot to use beans and peas instead[374] cast doubt on the adequacy of this arrangement. At the same time the publication in many parts of the Soviet Union of readers' letters denouncing the sending of consignments of matzot from abroad as 'a form of ideological blackmail'[375] indicated that these supplies had not been allowed to serve their intended purpose. In 1965, the baking of matzot was authorised in Moscow, Leningrad and Tbilisi.[376]

Meanwhile the admission in 1964 that there were then no more than 97 Jewish communities in the USSR as compared with the 150,[377] which had been stated to exist as recently as July, 1960,[378] demonstrated the inroads which the intensified anti-religious campaign had made into the practice of Judaism.

The post-Khrushchev leadership, more sensitive to world public opinion and concerned to counter past charges of anti-semitism, has appeared slightly less hostile in its attitude towards Judaism. Anti-semitism—along with other manifestations of nationalism—was condemned by Kosygin at Riga on July 18, 1965,[379] and also in a *Pravda* editorial in September, 1965.[380]

Token concessions to the Jewish community have been widely publicised. In July, 1965, Moscow's Chief Rabbi, Y. L. Levin, announced that the then Council for the Affairs of

Religious Cults had decided to allow the printing of religious calendars and 10,000 copies of a new prayer book. He added that the Council had also promised to remove all restrictions on the baking of matzot in Moscow and would allow the virtually defunct Moscow Yeshiva * to enrol 20 more pupils from all over the Soviet Union.[381] According to reports early in 1966, however, these promises had yet to be fulfilled.[383]

(e) BUDDHISM

Buddhism entered the Russian Empire in the form of Lamaism from Mongolia in the 17th century and was adopted by the Kalmyks and the Buryats,[384] Mongol peoples inhabiting areas along the Volga and around Lake Baikal respectively. By 1900 the number of *lamas* is said to have been as many as 16,000 and thereafter 'still greater'. Fifteen years later the number of *datsans* (Buddhist monastery temples) exceeded 40.[385]

At first the Communists adopted no special anti-Buddhist policy since these small Mongol peoples seemed suitable for exploitation to advance Soviet aims in the Far East. In January, 1926, the Soviet Government permitted a 'Congress of Soviet Buddhists' in Moscow, which produced an 'Appeal to the Buddhists of Mongolia, Tibet and India' and sent a telegram to the Dalai Lama praising the Soviet nationalities policy.[386] To further Buddhist-Communist collaboration certain Buryat intellectuals conceived a theory of 'Neo-Buddhism', alleging that Buddhism was actually a 'religion of atheism' and contained ideas on the emancipation of mankind corresponding to those of Marx and Lenin. This theory enjoyed official tolerance for a while, as did a 'renovationist' movement started by the *lamas* in the early years of Lenin's New Economic Policy in order to 'simplify divine service and make it more comprehensible to believers'.[387]

In 1928–1929 the 'developing offensive of Socialism along the whole front' brought with it a violent campaign against Buddhism. The Neo-Buddhist theories were condemned as 'most harmful' since they served 'to obliterate the class-consciousness of the revolutionary masses'.[388] 'Militant Godless' tried to prevent the celebration of Buddhist holidays, interfered with

* There were said to be only four pupils left at the seminary in 1965. Rabbi Levin denied reports that it had been closed altogether but said there had been a 'break' after the last graduating class.[382]

religious processions and closed *datsans*. By the end of 1929 the situation was so bad that the *lamas* and their followers prepared to emigrate *en masse* to Inner Mongolia.[389] The following year the Buryat branch of the League of Militant Godless had to be disbanded in face of intense local hostility aroused by anti-Buddhist excesses.[390]

There was then a lull until 1937, when a new campaign was launched. The *lamas* had apparently, like others, misunderstood the 1936 Constitution, thinking it contained a fundamental change in Communist policy towards religion. They were accused of 'spreading the most absurd rumours, calculated to deceive the workers: "the churches must be returned to the believers", "the *datsans* are now the property of the lamas", etc.'[391] In the summer of 1937 a group of *lamas* was 'unmasked and liquidated' for conspiring to conduct 'disruptive work in the collective farms' since 1929. Another group was 'liquidated' on charges of preparing to blow up bridges. The 'renovationist' Central Spiritual Council was denounced as the 'staff which organised, on the instruction of Japanese Fascism, the counter-revolutionary activity of the *lamas*'. This activity was now back-dated to the time of the Revolution when the *lamas* were said to have 'sought the help of the Mikado in the struggle against the Bolsheviks' and 'conducted their disgusting work for the Japanese secret service'. Thereafter they had 'outwardly "recognised" the Soviet régime but in reality are carrying on disruptive counter-revolutionary work'.[392] In particular they were accused of instructing believers that 'Japan is the bulwark of Buddhism' and hence that 'the intervention which the Japanese Fascists are preparing against the USSR ... [is] a "holy war" of the heavenly powers against the godless'. The *lamas*' description of the Russians as heretics was said to be 'one of their methods of inflaming chauvinism', the *lamas* 'exert every effort to compromise the Russians in the eyes of believers'. 'Every honest worker of Buryat-Mongolia and Kalmykia' was exhorted to 'understand that the *lamas* are a reactionary and class-hostile force, attempting to hinder and disrupt the triumphant course of Socialist construction in our country'.[393]

At the beginning of 1939 it was admitted: 'In Buryat-Mongolia the *lamas* still have considerable influence over the masses. ... Even some pedagogues and medical workers turn to the lamas as specialists in "Tibetan medicine".'[394] But, it was claimed, the *lamas* were being 'driven from their last positions'.[395]

During the war no public reference was made to the Soviet Buddhist war effort. In view of the earlier allegations of pro-Japanese sympathies it seems more likely that the Soviet Government did not encourage Buddhism as it did other religions. At the end of 1943 the Buddhist Kalmyks were deported *en masse* for alleged pro-German sympathies, and were only allowed to return to their re-established Autonomous Republic after 1957.

Since 1945 the fragmentary information available suggests that, broadly speaking, Buddhism has been exposed to similar conditions as other religious faiths. Successive Bandido-Hambo Lamas, who head the Central Buddhist Religious Board, have publicly associated themselves with Soviet propaganda campaigns in order to preserve their remaining institutions. In 1951, for example, Lobsan-Nima Darmayev, speaking on *Moscow Radio*, 'told of the atrocities being committed in Korea by the American gangsters and appealed to all Buddhists . . . to fight for peace throughout the world'.[396] Eshi-Derji Sharapov, who succeeded him in the autumn of 1956, went so far in the spring of 1958 as to denounce the Tibetan rising, expressing anger at 'imperialist activities' and 'the behaviour of the reactionaries'.[397] On his death Sharapov was described as 'a convinced partisan of world peace' and a resolute condemner of 'warmongers'.[398] (He was succeeded in September, 1963, by Zhamal Dorje Gomboev.[399])

These statements, while no doubt viewed by the Buddhist Council as a necessary sop to the Soviet Government, have not protected Buddhists from the familiar methods of the Party's anti-religious campaign. In 1960, for example, a former *lama* in Buryatia emphasised during his recantation published in the local Party daily that:

'Life itself shows clearly how wrong the teaching of the Buddhist religion is. I consider that honest labour for the good of mankind is the main thing in the life of every Soviet man.'[400]

Similarly a children's book, *The Secrets of Alkhani*, published in Buryatia in 1962, describes how, during an expedition by schoolchildren to follow in the tracks of heroes of the Civil War, 'the boy Tsyren, who had blindly trusted in the ancient beliefs, finds out how the *lamas* deceive the people'.[401]

The institutional losses suffered by Soviet Buddhists have been unusually severe. In 1960 it was claimed that whereas in 1916 there had been 36 *datsans* and 16,000 *lamas* in Buryatia, there were then in the Buryat Autonomous Republic and the Chita region no more than two *datsans* and 'a few dozen *lamas*'. In Tuva, where there had been 22 Buddhist temples and more than 4,000 *lamas* before the Revolution, there were only 100 *lamas* in 1960. (No mention was made of any Buddhist temples surviving in this area.[402]) The total number of lamas in the Soviet Union in 1962 was later given as 'about 300.'[403]

In 1961 an account of conditions in Buryatia by a post-graduate student at Moscow University told how hundreds of believers were still going 'on horseback, in buses and even in aeroplanes' to the Ivolginsk *datsan*—'the last of the 36 Buddhist temples which were inherited from old Buryatia'. Complaining of the continuing prevalence in various areas of rags with Buddhist prayers inscribed on them flying from poles above people's houses, the writer declared:

'The Buddhist poles will not fall down by themselves. A strong, fresh wind cleansing the air of the corruption of religious obscurantism can bring them down.'[404]

SOURCES

1. *Mir Islama,* 1913, No. XI, pp. 269–271.
2. *Moscow Radio* in Arabic, July 5, 1959.
3. *Tashkent Radio,* January 19, 1959.
4. Gordienko, p. 26.
5. *B.S.E.,* 1st edn., Vol. on the USSR, p. 1789.
6. *Voprosy Filosofi,* 1957, No. 5, p. 224.
7. Marx and Engels, *Sochineniya,* Vol. XXI, p. 484.
8. *RSFSR Laws,* 1917–1918, 6: appendix 2.
9. Smirnov, p. 132.
10. *RSFSR Laws,* 1917–1918, 17: 243.
11. Lenin, *Sochineniya,* Vol. 29, p. 151.
12. *Smirnov,* p. 135.
13. Stalin, *Works,* Vol. 4, p. 409.
14. *Ibid.,* p. 415.
15. Gidulyanov, 1926 edn., pp. 61–62.
16. *RSFSR Laws,* 1921, 39: 206.
17. Smirnov, p. 138.
18. *Ibid.,* pp. 139–140.
19. Samursky, p. 136.
20. *B.S.E.,* 1st edn., Vol. 61, p. 855.
21. Smirnov, p. 149.
22. *Ibid.,* p. 236.
23. *KPSS v Resolyutsiyakh,* Vol. I, p. 744.
24. *Ibid.,* Vol. II, p. 53.
25. Smirnov, p. 145.
26. *Ibid.,* p. 158.

27. *Sovetskoe Stroitelstvo,* 1929, No. 5, p. 164.
28. *Revolyutsiya i Natsionalnosti,* 1930, No. 2, p. 38.
29. *Antireligioznik,* 1931, No. 11, p. 72.
30. Smirnov, p. 195.
31. *B.S.E.,* 1st edn., Vol. 29, pp. 371–372.
32. *Ibid.,* p. 393.
33. *Ibid.,* p. 394.
34. *Ibid.,* p. 396.
35. Smirnov, p. 165.
36. *Ibid.,* p. 164.
37. *Ibid.,* pp. 202–203.
38. *Ibid.,* p. 167.
39. *Ibid.,* p. 167.
40. *Ibid.,* pp. 239–240.
41. Oleshchuk, *Borba Tserkvi Protiv Naroda,* p. 50.
42. *Ibid.,* p. 45.
43. *Ibid.,* p. 87.
44. *Pravda,* July 9, 1937.
45. *Oleshchuk, op. cit.,* p. 89.
46. *Bolshevik,* 1938, No. 30.
47. *Sovetskaya Yustitsiya,* 1938, No. 23–24.
48. *Religious Communities in the Soviet Union,* p. 3.
49. *B.S.E.,* 1st edn., Vol. 38, p. 634.
50. *Ibid.,* Vol. 61, p. 855.
51. *Religious Communities in the Soviet Union,* p. 3.
52. *Soviet War News,* October 24, 1942.
53. *Soviet Monitor,* October 27, 1943.
54. *Soviet Monitor,* May 28, 1944.
55. *B.S.E.,* 1st edn., Vol. on the USSR, p. 1789.
56. *Spasov,* p. 27.
57. *Moscow Radio,* December 16, 1944.
58. *Alger Républicain,* October 7, 1947.
59. Tubert, pp. 127–128.
60. *Alger Républicain,* December 20, 1950.
61. *Izvestiya,* October 17, 1947.
62. *Moscow Radio* in Arabic, November 29, 1952.
63. *Kommunist Tadzhikistana,* October 12, 1960.
64. *Akher Sa'a* (the Cairo newspaper), March 26, 1955.
65. *L'Afrique et L'Asie,* 1960, No. 4.
66. *Nauka i Religiya,* 1960, No. 7, p. 26.
67. *Turkmenskaya Iskra,* February 27, 1957.
68. *Nauka i Religiya,* 1964, No. 2, p. 55.
69. *L'Afrique et L'Asie,* 1960, No. 4.
70. *B.S.E.,* 2nd edn., Vol. 21, p. 474.
71. *Knizhnaya Letopis,* 1957, No. 39, p. 90.
72. *Knizhnaya Letopis,* 1958, No. 2, p. 105.
73. *Kommunist Tadzhikistana,* August 20, 1954.
74. *Nauka i Religiya,* 1960, No. 3, p. 85.
75. *Nauka i Religiya,* 1961, No. 5, pp. 9–13.
76. *Nauka i Religiya,* 1962, No. 5, p. 23.
77. *Nauka i Religiya,* 1963, No. 8, pp. 88–89.
78. *Kommunist Tadzhikistana,* October 17, 1963.
79. *Nauka i Religiya,* 1962, No. 4, pp. 94–95.
80. *Nauka i Religiya,* 1960, No. 5, pp. 44–46.
81. *Sovetskaya Kirgiziya,* April 28, 1960.
82. *Kommunist Tadzhikistana,* March 17, 1961.
83. *Turkmenskaya Iskra,* November 23, 1963.

84. *Sovetskaya Kirgiziya*, September 17, 1959.
85. *Sovetskaya Kirgiziya*, January 5, 1962.
86. *Nauka i Religiya*, 1963, No. 9, p. 75.
87. *Ibid.*, p. 76.
88. *Nauka i Religiya*, 1966, No. 1, p. 72.
89. *Nauka i Religiya*, 1965, No. 10, p. 56.
90. *Pravda Vostoka*, February 23, 1965.
91. *Sovetskaya Kultura*, July 16, 1966.
92. *Bakinsky Rabochi*, July 5, 1963.
93. *Kazakhstanskaya Pravda*, August 28, 1963.
94. *Kommunist Uzbekistana*, 1963, No. 9, p. 64.
95. *Kommunist*, 1964, No. 1, p. 40.
96. *Pravda Vostoka*, October 22, 1965.
    Pravda Vostoka, July 26, 1965.
97. *Kommunist*, 1964, No. 1, p. 40.
98. *Partiinaya Zhizn Kazakhstana*, 1964, No. 1, p. 39.
99. *Nauka i Religiya*, 1965, No. 9, p. 85.
100. *Pravda Vostoka*, February 23, 1965.
101. *Nauka i Religiya*, May 5, 1966, p. 23.
102. Anderson, *People, Church and State in Modern Russia*, p. 8.
103. Evans, p. 32.
104. *Ibid.*
105. *Ibid.*, pp. 33, 27.
106. *Annuario Pontificio* (hereafter cited as *A.P.*), 1925, p. 761.
107. *Ibid.*, p. 237.
108. *Ibid.*, 1931, p. 185.
109. Evans, p. 70.
110. *A.P.*, 1925, p. 171.
111. Anderson, *op. cit.*, pp. 57–58.
112. Mikhnevich, p. 241.
113. *A.P.*, 1926, p. 173; 1940, p. 1181.
114. *A.P.*, 1923, p. 244.
115. Anderson, *op. cit.*, p. 58.
116. *A.P.*, 1931, p. 185.
117. Evans, p. 70.
118. Timasheff, p. 30.
119. McCullagh, pp. 201, 254.
120. Timasheff, p. 30.
121. Evans, p. 70.
122. *A.P.*, 1926, p. 257.
123. Mikhnevich, pp. 240–241.
124. Maynard, p. 363.
125. *Ibid.*
126. *Ibid.*
127. *Ibid.*
128. *Mikhnevich*, p. 242.
129. Evans, p. 71.
130. Mikhnevich, p. 241.
131. Evans, p. 73.
132. Anderson, *op. cit.*, p. 103.
133. Oleshchuk, *op. cit.*, p. 55.
134. Curtiss, p. 307.
135. *First Victims of Communism*, p. 101.
136. *A.P.*, 1947, p. 22.
137. *First Victims of Communism*, p. 29.
138. *Ibid.*, p. 104.
139. *Vaitiekunas*, p. 54.
140. *Ibid.*, p. 55.
141. *Ibid.*, p. 58.
142. *Ibid.*, p. 60.
143. *Ibid.*, p. 61.
144. *Religious Communities in the Soviet Union*, p. 3.
145. Maynard, p. 377.
146. Evans, p. 94.
147. Vaitiekunas, p. 57.
148. *Malaya Sovetskaya Entsiklopediya*, 3rd edn., Vol. 3, p. 749.
149. Vaitiekunas, p. 64.

150. *Soviet Monitor*, No. 11, 980, October 20, 1950.
151. *Soviet Monitor*, October 3, 1951.
152. *First Victims of Communism*, p. 30.
153. *Ibid.*, p. 106 .
154. *Ibid.*, p. 33.
155. *Ibid.*, p. 107.
156. *Ibid.*, p. 33.
157. *Ibid.*
158. Bolshakoff, p. 140.
159. *First Victims of Communism*, p. 34.
160. *Lvovskaya Pravda*, March 1, 1946; *Zh.M.P.*, 1946, No. 4, p. 36.
161. *First Victims of Communism*, pp. 34–36.
162. *Ukrainian Bulletin*, March 15, 1954.
163. *L'Osservatore Romano*, No. 288, December 9–10, 1946; *First Victims of Communism*, p. 46.
164. *First Victims of Communism*, pp. 46–47.
165. *Ibid.*
166. *Ibid.*, p. 36.
167. *Zh.M.P.*, 1948, No. 10, p. 12.
168. *First Victims of Communism*, p. 106.
169. *Ibid.*, p. 108.
170. *Ibid.*, p. 38.
171. *Ibid.*, pp. 39–40.
172. *Ibid.*, p. 38.
173. *Ibid.*, pp. 40, 42.
174. *Ibid.*, pp. 42, 108.
175. *Ibid.*
176. *Zh.M.P.*, 1946, No. 4, p. 5.
177. *Ibid.*
178. *Ibid.*, p. 6.
179. *Ibid.*
180. *Ibid.*, p. 9.
181. *Ibid.*, pp. 22–23.
182. *Ibid.*, p. 24.
183. *Ibid.*, p. 26.
184. *Ibid.*, p. 27.
185. *Ibid.*, p. 28.
186. *Ibid.*, p. 31.
187. *Ibid.*, pp. 10–11.
188. *Ibid.*, p. 34.
189. *First Victims of Communism*, p. 109.
190. *Zh.M.P.*, 1948, No. 10, pp. 12–14.
191. *Ibid.*, p. 10.
192. *Ibid.*, p. 9.
193. *First Victims of Communism*, p. 106.
194. *Ibid.*, pp. 48–49.
195. *Ibid.*, p. 50.
196. *Ibid.*, pp. 52–54.
197. *Ibid.*, pp. 54–55.
198. *Ibid.*, pp. 55–56.
199. *Ibid.*; A.P., 1948, p. 1220.
200. *B.S.E.*, 2nd edn., Vol. 10, p. 118.
201. *Ibid.*
202. *Izvestiya*, March 15, 1952.
203. *Ogonek*, 1952, No. 15, p. 27.
204. *Pravda*, March 17, 1952.
205. *Izvestiya*, March 18, 1952.
206. *Tass in Russian for Abroad*, December 26, 1955.
207. *Sovetskaya Litva*, October 10, 1959.
208. *Sovetskaya Latviya*, March 11, 1964.
209. *Knizhnaya Letopis*, 1963, No. 45, p. 76; *Ibid.*, No. 42, p. 84.
210. *Nauka i Religiya*, 1960, No. 11, p. 87.
211. *Nauka i Religiya*, 1963, No. 6, p. 73.
212. *Nauka i Religiya*, 1961, No. 1, p. 81.
213. *Nauka i Religiya*, 1963, No. 6, p. 73.
214. *Izvestiya*, May 12, 1964.
215. *Komsomolskaya Pravda*, August 7, 1962.

216. *Sovetskaya Latviya,* September 17, 1959.
217. *Sovetskaya Litva,* November 19, 1959.
218. *Pravda,* January 14, 1962.
219. *Komsomolskaya Pravda,* August 7, 1962.
220. *Ogonek,* 1963, No. 46, pp. 30–31.
221. *Za Rubezhom,* 1962, No. 43.
   Literaturnaya Gazeta, December 8, 1962.
222. *The Times,* February 12, 1963.
223. *Izvestiya,* June 5, 1963.
224. *Kommunist,* 1964, No. 15, p. 88.
225. *Voprosy Filosofii,* 1965, No. 8, p. 115.
226. *Sovetskaya Litva,* December 19, 1963.
227. *Ibid.*
228. *Voprosi Istorii CPSU,* 1965, No. 10, pp. 13, 15.
229. *Sovetskaya Litva,* October 8, 1966.
   Sovetskaya Litva, October 9, 1966.
230. A.P., 1966.
231. *British Lithuanian Council Press Service,* September, 1963.
232. *The Tablet,* July 3, 1965.
233. *Moscow Radio* in English for North America, September 12, 1961.
234. *Moscow Radio* in English for North America, April 27, 1960.
235. *Moscow Radio* in English for North America, November 20, 1960.
236. Bolshakoff, pp. 17–18.
237. *B.S.E.,* 1st edn., Vol. 4, p. 679; Vol. 50, p. 656.
238. Bolshakoff, pp. 117–120.

239. *B.S.E.,* 2nd edn., Vol. 4, p. 215.
240. *KPSS v Rezolyutsiyakh,* Vol. I, p. 48.
241. Bolshakoff, p. 119.
242. *Ibid.,* pp. 119–120.
243. *RSFSR Laws,* 1917, 17: 192.
244. Evans, p. 62.
245. *KPSS v Rezolyutsiyakh,* Vol. I, p. 744.
246. *Ibid.,* Vol. II, p. 52.
247. Evans, p. 63.
248. *B.S.E.,* 1st edn., Vol. 4, p. 679.
249. *Ibid.,* Vol. 23, p. 811.
250. Evans, p. 63.
251. *B.S.E.,* 1st edn., Vol. 23, p. 811.
252. Bolshakoff, p. 120.
253. *B.S.E.,* 1st edn., Vol. 23, p. 810.
254. Maynard, p. 361.
255. Oleshchuk, *op. cit.,* pp. 40–41.
256. Anderson, *op. cit.,* p. 86.
257. Evans, p. 63.
258. Oleshchuk, *op. cit.,* p. 39.
259. *Ibid.,* p. 40.
260. *B.S.E.,* 1st edn., Vol. 23, p. 811.
261. Oleshchuk, *op. cit.,* p. 40.
262. *Religious Communities in the Soviet Union,* p. 3.
263. Evans, pp. 142–144.
264. *Ibid.,* pp. 144–146.
265. *B.S.E.,* 1st edn., Vol. 50, p. 658.
266. Bolshakoff, p. 121.
267. *Izvestiya,* November 10, 1944.
268. Bolshakoff, pp. 121–122.
269. *Bratsky Vestnik* (hereafter cited as *B.V.*), 1947, No. 2, p. 61.
270. *Ibid.,* No. 1, pp. 13–15.
271. *Conference in Defence of Peace,* pp. 77–78.

272. *B.V.*, 1948, No. 1, pp. 6–7.
273. Bolshakoff, p. 128.
274. *B.V.*, 1954, No. 3–4.
275. *Leningradskaya Pravda*, February 27, 1964.
276. *B.V.*, 1963, No. 3, p. 65, 70, 71.
277. *Kazakhstanskaya Pravda*, June 2, 1963.
278. *Nauka i Religiya*, 1963, No. 4, p. 9.
279. *Sovetskaya Moldaviya*, November 27, 1963.
280. *Nauka i Religiya*, 1961, Nos. 2 and 3.
281. *Sovetskaya Kirgiziya*, May 14, 1961.
282. *Sovetskaya Latviya*, February 9, 1964.
283. *Nauka i Religiya*, 1963, No. 4, p. 8.
284. *Nauka i Religiya*, 1963, No. 5, p. 45.
285. *Nauki i Religiya*, 1963, No. 9, p. 77.
286. *Izvestiya*, January 23, 1962.
287. *Pravda Vostoka*, October 3, 1962.
288. *Pravda Vostoka*, February 29, 1964.
289. *Nauka i Religiya*, 1964, No. 2, p. 8.
290. *Sovetskaya Rossiya*, June 9, 1963.
291. *Sovetskaya Moldaviya*, June 7, 1964.
292. Fedorenko, 'Sects, their Faith and Deeds', p. 167.
293. *Pravda Ukrainy*, October 4, 1966.
294. *Pravda*, January 12, 1963.
295. *Sovetskaya Belorussiya*, May 12, 1963.
296. *Pravda Vostoka*, November 15, 1963.
297. *Pravda o Khristianskikh Sektakh*, p. 73.

298. *Ibid.*, p. 114.
299. *Sovetskaya Yustitsiya*, 1964, No. 9, pp. 26–27.
300. *B.V.*, 1963, No. 6, p. 36.
301. *Ibid.*, p. 52.
302. *Ibid.*, p. 19.
303. *Ibid.*, p. 14.
304. *Ibid.*, p. 55.
305. *World Christian Handbook*, p. 221; *Current Developments*, August/September, 1962, p. 5.
306. Fedorenko, p. 166.
307. *Izvestiya*, June 5, 1966.
308. *Nauka i Religiya*, 1966, No. 7, p. 25.
309. *Izvestiya*, June 5, 1966.
310. *Nauka i Religiya*, 1966, No. 7, p. 24.
     Nauka i Religiya, 1966, No. 9, p. 24.
311. *Uchitelskaya Gazeta*, August 23, 1966.
312. *Pravda*, February 19, 1966.
313. *Pravda Ukrainy*, October 4, 1966.
314. *Sovetskaya Kirgiziya*, March 18, 1966.
315. *Izvestiya*, August 30, 1966.
316. *Izvestiya*, June 5, 1966.
317. *Selskaya Zhizn*, July 17, 1966.
318. *Nauka i Religiya*, 1962, No. 7, p. 50.
     Kommunist, 1960, No. 9, p. 114.
319. *Nauka i Religiya*, 1961, No. 10, p. 47.
320. *Sovetskaya Rossiya*, December 22, 1962.
321. *Kommunisticheskoe Prosveshchenie*, August 5, 1931, pp. 33–34.
322. *Osteuropa*, October, 1936, No. 1.
323. *Tass in English*, April 2, 1961.

324. *World Christian Handbook*, p. 220; *Current Developments*, p. 5.
325. *Ibid.*
326. *Sovetskaya Estoniya*, August 14, 1963.
327. *Yearbook of International Organisations*, 1954–55, p. 277.
328. Fedorenko, p. 191.
329. *Moscow Home Service*, June 28, 1963.
330. *Sovetskaya Latviya*, November 13, 1963.
331. *Nauka i Religiya*, 1963, No. 5, p. 26.
332. *Der Mennonit*, 1957, No. 7, p. 86.
333. *Nauka i Religiya*, 1963, No. 5, p. 27.
334. *B.V.*, 1963, No. 6, p. 50.
335. *Ibid.*, p. 42.
336. *Literaturnaya Gazeta*, October 30, 1958.
337. *Nauka i Religiya*, 1962, No. 11, p. 57.
338. Fedorenko, p. 136.
339. *B.S.E.*, 2nd edn., Vol. 15, p. 378.
340. Stalin, *Works*, Vol. 2, p. 310.
341. *Bezbozhnik*, September 22, 1929.
342. Smirnov, pp. 159–160.
343. Oleshchuk, *op. cit.*, p. 59.
344. *Ibid.*, p. 60.
345. *Ibid.*, pp. 61–62.
346. Schwarz, p. 115.
347. Oleschuk, *op. cit.*, p. 61.
348. *Religious Communities in the Soviet Union*, p. 4; Schwartz, p. 114.
349. *Pravda*, November 14, 1942.
350. *Izvestiya*, March 18, 1955.
351. *Izvestiya*, November 29, 1956.

352. *Moscow Radio*, October 18, 1958.
353. *Tass for Abroad*, January 10, 1957.
354. *New York Herald Tribune*, August 6, 1962.
355. *Nauka i Religiya*, 1962, No. 12, p. 31.
356. *Sovetskaya Kirgiziya*, May 8, 1962; *Nauka i Religiya*, 1962, No. 8, p. 27.
357. *Nauka i Religiya*, 1963, No. 2, p. 28.
358. *Nauka i Religiya*, 1961, No. 5, p. 91.
359. *Lvovskaya Pravda*, February 16 and March 9, 1962.
360. *Sunday Telegraph*, December 30, 1962.
361. *Kommunist Moldavii*, 1961, No. 7.
362. *Nauka i Religiya*, 1959, No. 4 (December), p. 35; *Trud*, January 19, 1962; *Trud*, March 11, 1964.
363. *Leningradskaya Pravda*, November 11, 1961.
364. *Nauka i Religiya*, 1962, No. 4, pp. 34–36; *Nauka i Religiya*, 1962, No. 9, pp. 26–29.
365. *Daily Worker*, March 25, 1964.
366. *L'Humanité*, March 25, 1964.
367. *L'Unità*, March 28 and 29, 1964.
368. *Pravda*, April 4, 1964.
369. *New York Herald Tribune*, June 24, 1962.
370. *Jews in Eastern Europe*, September, 1963, p. 38.
371. *Jews in Eastern Europe*, December, 1962, p. 35.
372. *New York Herald Tribune*, July 17, 1963.
373. *Daily Worker*, March 19, 1964.

374. *Jewish Chronicle*, April 3, 1964.
375. *Kommunist Tadzhikistana,* March 15, 1964; *Pravda Vostoka,* March 17, 1964; *Sovetskaya Belorussiya,* March 22, 1964; *Sovetskaya Moldaviya,* March 26, 1964; *Sovetskaya Latviya,* March 27, 1964.
376. *Daily Worker,* March 11, 1965.
377. *Moscow Radio* in English for North America, January 10, 1964.
378. *Moscow Radio* in English for North America, July 22, 1960.
379. *Pravda,* July 19, 1965.
380. *Pravda,* September 5, 1965.
380. *Pravda,* September 5, 1965.
381. *Moscow Radio* in English for North America, August 23, 1965.
382. *Jewish Chronicle,* June 25, 1965.
383. *Jewish Chronicle,* January 11, 1966. *Jewish Chronicle,* February 25, 1966.
384. Oleshchuk, *op. cit.*, p. 63.

385. *Ibid.*
386. Klimovich, p. 68.
387. Oleshchuk, *op. cit.*, p. 65.
388. *Antireligioznik,* 1930, No. 7, p. 22.
389. Oleshchuk, *op. cit.*, p. 65.
390. *Antireligioznik,* 1930, No. 8–9, pp. 55–56.
391. Oleshchuk, *op. cit.*, p. 66.
392. *Ibid.,* p. 65.
393. *Ibid.,* pp. 66–67.
394. *Ibid.,* p. 104.
395. *Ibid.,* p. 65.
396. *Conference in Defence of Peace,* pp. 216–217.
397. *Moscow Radio* in Burmese, April 4, 1959.
398. *Tass in Russian for Abroad,* March 12, 1963.
399. *Tass in Russian for Abroad,* September 25, 1963.
400. *Pravda Buryatii,* January 30, 1960.
401. *Nauka i Religiya,* 1962, No. 12, p. 88.
402. *Nauka i Religiya,* 1960, No. 6, p. 23.
403. *Kratky Nauchno-Ateisti-chesky Slovar,*1964, p. 312.
404. *Nauka i Religiya,* 1961, No. 7, p. 32.

BIBLIOGRAPHY

L'Afrique et L'Asie, quarterly published by Centre Des Hautes Etudes, 13, Rue de Four, Paris, 6.

Akher Sa'a, weekly news magazine published by Dar Akhbar El-Yon, Cairo.

Alger Républicain, an Algerian Left-Wing newspaper, under FLN management since April, 1964.

Amosov, N. K., *Proiskhozhdenie i Klassovaya Sushchnost Khristianstva* (Origin and Class Essence of Christianity), State Publishing House of Cultural-Enlightenment Literature, Moscow, 1952.

Anderson, Paul B., *People, Church and State in Modern Russia*, Student Movement Christian Press, London, 1944.

Annuario Pontificio, official yearbook, Tipografia Poliglotta Vaticana, Rome (cited as A.P.).

Antireligioznik (The Anti-Religious), periodical, organ (1924–1941) of the Godless League.

Bakinsky Rabochy (Baku Worker), newspaper, organ of the Central and Baku Committees of the Communist Party of Azerbaidzhan.

Bezbozhnik (The Godless), newspaper, organ (1922–1934, 1938–1941) of the Godless League.

Bezbozhnik (The Godless), periodical, organ (1923, 1932–1941) of the Godless League.

Bolshakoff, Serge, *Russian Non-Conformity*, Westminster Press, Philadelphia, 1950.

Bolshaya Sovetskaya Entsiklopediya (Large Soviet Encyclopaedia), 1st Edition, 56 volumes, with supplementary volume on USSR, Moscow, 1926–1947; 2nd edition, 51 volumes, Moscow, 1949–1958 (cited as B.S.E.).

Bolshevik, former political and economic journal of the Soviet Communist Party.

Bratsky Vestnik (Brothers' Herald), periodical, organ of the All-Union Council of Evangelical Christian-Baptists (cited as B.V.).

British Lithuanian Council Press Service, bulletin put out by the British Lithuanian Council in London.

Conference in Defence of Peace of All Churches and Religious Associations in the USSR, published by the Moscow Patriarchate, 1952 cited as *Conference in Defence of Peace*).

Curie, Eve, *Journey Among Warriors*, Garden City, N.Y., 1943.

Current Developments in the East European Churches, periodical, published by the World Council of Churches, Geneva (cited as *Current Developments*).

Curtiss, John Shelton, *The Russian Church and the Soviet State,* Little, Brown and Company, Boston, 1953.

Derevensky Bezbozhnik (The Village Godless), periodical (1926–1941) of the Godless League.

Discussione, weekly newspaper of the Italian Christian Democrat Party.

Enisherlov, M. (ed.), *Voinstvuyushchee Bezbozhie v SSSR Za 15 Let* (Fifteen years of Militant Godlessness in the USSR), Moscow, 1932.

Evans, Stanley, *The Churches in the USSR,* Cobbett Publishing Co. Ltd., London, 1943.

Fedorenko, F., *Sects, their Faith and Deeds,* Publishing House of Political Literature, Moscow, 1965.

First Victims of Communism, White Book on religious persecution in the Ukraine, Analecta OSBM, Rome, 1953.

Gidulyanov, P. V. (ed.), *Otdelenie Tserkvi ot Gosudarstva—Polny Sbornik Dekretov RSFSR i SSSR, Instruktsiy, Tsirkulyarov i.t.d.* (The Separation of the Church from the State—Complete Collection of Decrees of the RSFSR and USSR, Instructions, Circulars, etc.), Moscow, 1924; revised edition, 1926.

Gordienko, A. A., *Sozdanie Sovetskoi Natsionalnoi Gosudarstvennosti v Srednei Azii* (The Creation of Soviet National Statehood in Central Asia), State Publishing House of Juridical Literature, Moscow, 1959.

Gurian, Waldeman (ed.), *The Soviet Union, Background, Ideology, Reality,* Notre Dame, Indiana, 1951.

Gurvich, G. S., *Istoriya Sovetskoi Konstitutsii* (History of the Soviet Constitution), Moscow, 1923.

Izvestiya (News), newspaper, organ of the Presidium of the Supreme Soviet (formerly Central Executive Committee) of the USSR.

Jews in Eastern Europe, periodical survey published by European Jewish Publications Ltd., London.

The Jewish Chronicle, weekly newspaper published in London.

Kazakhstanskaya Pravda (Kazakhstan Truth), newspaper, organ of the Central Committee of the Communist Party of Kazakhstan.

L. I. Klimovich, *Sotsialisticheskoe Stroitelstvo na Vostoke i Religiya* (Socialist Construction in the East and Religion), Moscow–Leningrad, 1929.

Knizhnaya Letopis (Book Chronicle), bibliographical journal of the All-Union Book Chamber, Moscow.

Kolonitsky, P., *Moral Kommunisticheskaya i Moral Religioznaya* (Communist Morality and Religious Morality), 'Young Guard' Publishing House, Moscow, 1952.

Kommunist (The Communist), formerly *Bolshevik*, periodical, organ of the Central Committee of the Communist Party of the Soviet Union.

Kommunist Moldavii (Communist of Moldavia) periodical, organ of the Central Committee of the Communist Party of Moldavia.

Kommunist Tadzhikistana (Communist of Tadzhikistan) newspaper, organ of the Central and Dushanbe Town Committees of the Communist Party of Tadzhikistan and of the Supreme Soviet of the Tadzhik SSR.

Kommunist Ukrainy (Communist of the Ukraine), periodical, organ of the Central Committee of the Communist Party of the Ukraine.

Kommunist Uzbekistana (Communist of Uzbekistan), periodical, organ of the Central Committee of the Communist Party of Uzbekistan.

Kommunisticheskoe Prosveshchenie (Communist Enlightenment), periodical, organ of RSFSR People's Commissariat for Education (1920–1936).

Komsomolsky Rabotnik (Young Communist Worker) periodical, organ (formerly) of the Komsomol Central Committee.

Komsomolskaya Pravda (Young Communist Truth), newspaper, organ of the Central and Moscow Komsomol Committees.

Konstitutii Soyuza SSR i Soyuznykh Respublik (Constitutions of the USSR and the Union Republics), Moscow, 1932.

KPSS V Rezolyutsiyakh i Resheniyakh Sezdov, Konferentsiy i Plenumov Tsk (The CPSU in Resolutions and Decisions of Congresses, Conferences and Plenums of the CC), 7th Edition, 3 volumes, State Publishing House of Political Literature, Moscow, 1954.

Kratky Filosofsky Slovar (Short Philosophical Dictionary), 4th Edition, State Publishing House of Political Literature, Moscow, 1954.

Kratky Nauchno-Ateistichesky Slovar (Short Scientific-Atheist Dictionary) *Nauka* Publishing House, Moscow, 1964.

Lenin, V. I., *Socineniya* (Works), 4th Edition, 35 volumes, Marx-Engels-Lenin Institute, Moscow, 1941–1950.

Leningradskaya Pravda (Leningrad Truth), newspaper, organ of the Leningrad Regional Party Committee and the Leningrad City Soviet.

Literaturnaya Gazeta (Literary Gazette), newspaper, organ of the Board of the Union of Writers of the USSR.

Lvovskaya Pravda (Lvov Truth) newspaper, organ of the Lvov Regional Party Committee.

Lyons, E., *Assignment to Utopia*, New York, 1937.

Malaya Sovetskaya Entsiklopediya (Small Soviet Encyclopaedia), 3rd Edition, 10 volumes, Moscow, 1958–1960.

Marx, K. and Engels, F., *Sochineniya* (Works), 1st edition, 29 volumes, Marx-Engels-Lenin Institute, Moscow, 1938–1948.

Maynard, Sir John, *The Russian Peasant and Other Studies*, Victor Gollancz Ltd., London, 1943.

McCullagh, Francis, *The Bolshevik Persecution of Christianity*, London, 1924.

Der Mennonit, periodical, published by the International Mennonite Community, Frankfurt-on-Main.

Mikhnevich, D. E., *Ocherki iz Istorii Katolicheskoi Reaktsii* (Outlines of the History of Catholic Reaction), Publishing House of the USSR Academy of Sciences, Moscow, 1953.

Mir Islama (The World of Islam), periodical (1912–1917) of the Imperial Society of Oriental Studies, St. Petersburg.

Molodoi Kommunist (Young Communist), formerly *Molodoi Bolshevik*, periodical, organ of the Komsomol Central Committee.

Nauka i Religiya (Science and Religion) 'popular scientific and atheistic journal', published by the All-Union 'Znanie' ('Knowledge') Society, Moscow.

Nauka i Zhizn (Science and Life), periodical, published by the All-Union 'Znanie' Society, Moscow.

Ogonek (The Light), illustrated periodical published by *Pravda*.

O Konstitutsii Soyuza SSR (About the Constitution of the USSR), Party Publishing House of the Party Central Committee, 1937.

Oleshchuk, F., *Borba Tserkvi Protiv Naroda* (The Struggle of the Church Against the People), State Publishing House of Political Literature, Moscow, 1939.

Oleshchuk, F., *O. Preodolenii Religioznykh Perezhitkov* (On Overcoming Religious Survivals), Moscow, 1941.

Orleansky, N. (comp), *Zakon O Religioznykh Obedineniyakh RSFSR i Deistvuyushchie Zakony, Instruktsii, c Otdelnymi Kommentariyami* (The Law on Religious Associations in the RSFSR and Operative Laws and Instructions, with Commentaries), Moscow, 1930.

Osteuropa, specialised journal published monthly by the German Society for East European Studies, Stuttgart.

Partiinaya Zhizn (Party Life), journal of the Central Committee of the Soviet Communist Party.

Partiinaya Zhizn Kazakhstana (Party Life of Kazakhstan), periodical, organ of the Central Committee of the Communist Party of Kazakhstan.

Patriarkh Sergei i Ego Dukhovnoe Nasledstvo (Patriarch Sergei and His Spiritual Legacy), Moscow Patriarchate, Moscow, 1947 (cited as *Patriarkh Sergei*).

Pechat SSSR (The USSR Press), an annual statistical review published by the All-Union Book Chamber, Moscow.

Pod Znamenem Marksizma (Under the Banner of Marxism), periodical, published (1922–1948) by *Pravda*.

Podyachikh, P. G., Vsesoyuznaya Perepis Naseleniya 1939 (The All-Union Population Census of 1939), State Statistical Publishing House, Moscow, 1953.

Pravda (Truth), newspaper, organ of the Central Committee of the Communist Party of the Soviet Union.

Pravda Buryatii (Truth of Buryatia), newspaper, organ of the Buryat Regional Party Committee.

Pravda o Khristianskikh Sektakh (The Truth About Christian Sects), The Military Publishing House of the USSR Ministry of Defence, Moscow, 1963.

Pravda o Religi v Rosii (The Truth About Religion in Russia), Moscow Patriarchate, Moscow, 1942 (cited as *Pravda o Religii*).

Pravda Ukrainy (Truth of the Ukraine), newspaper, organ of the Central Committee of the Communist Party of the Ukraine and of the Supreme Soviet and Council of Ministers of the Ukrainian SSR.

Pravda Vostoka (Truth of the East), newspaper, organ of the Central Committee of the Communist Party of Uzbekistan and of the Supreme Soviet and Council of Ministers of the Uzbek SSSR.

Propagandist, periodical, organ (formerly) of the Central and Moscow Committees of the Communist Party of the Soviet Union.

Religious Communities in the Soviet Union, Press Department of the Soviet Embassy, London, August, 1941.

Revolyutsiya i Natsionalnosti (The Revolution and the Nationalities), periodical, organ (formerly) of the Council of Nationalities of the Central Executive Committee of the USSR and the Communist Academy.

Revolyutsiya i Tserkov (The Revolution and the Church), periodical, organ (1919–1924) of the Commissariat of Justice.

RSFSR Laws:

1917–38: *Sobranie Uzakoneniy i Rasporyazheniy Raboche-Krestyanskogo Pravitelstva Rossiyskoi Sovetskoi Federativnoi Sotsialisticheskoi Respubliki* (Collection of Statutes and Orders of the Worker-Peasant Government of the Russian Soviet Federative Socialist Republic), People's Commissariat of Justice of the RSFSR, Moscow.

Russky Golos (The Russian Voice), newspaper, organ of the American Committee for the Liberation of the Peoples of Russia, New York.

N. Samursky, *Dagestan* (Daghestan), Moscow, 1925.

Schwartz, Solomon M., *The Jews in the Soviet Union*, Syracuse University Press, 1951.

Selskaya Zhizn (Rural Life), newspaper, organ of the Central Committee of the Soviet Communist Party.

Smirnov, N. A., *Ocherki Istorii Izucheniya Islama v SSSR* (Outlines of the History of the Study of Islam in the USSR), Publishing House of the USSR Academy of Sciences, Moscow, 1954.

Sovetskaya Belorussiya (Soviet Byelorussiya), newspaper, organ of the Central Committee of the Communist Party of Byelorussia and of the Supreme Soviet and Council of Ministers of the Byelorussian SSR.

Sovetskaya Estoniya (Soviet Estonia), newspaper, organ of the Central Committee of the Communist Party of Estonia and of the Supreme Soviet and Council of Ministers of the Estonian SSR.

Sovetskaya Kirgiziya (Soviet Kirghizia), newspaper, organ of the Central and Frunze Committees of the Communist Party of Kirghizia and of the Supreme Soviet and Council of Ministers of the Kirghiz SSR.

Sovetskaya Latviya (Soviet Latvia), newspaper, organ of the Central Committee of the Communist Party of Latvia and of the Supreme Soviet of the Latvian SSR.

Sovetskaya Litva (Soviet Lithuania), newspaper, organ of the Central Committee of the Communist Party of Lithuania and of the Presidium of the Supreme Soviet and the Council of Ministers of the Lithuanian SSR.

Sovetskaya Moldaviya (Soviet Moldavia), newspaper, organ of the Central Committee of the Communist Party of Moldavia and of the Supreme Soviet of the Moldavian SSR.

Sovetskaya Rossiya (Soviet Russia), newspaper, organ of the Buro for the RSFSR of the Central Committee of the Soviet Communist Party and of the RSFSR Council of Ministers.

Sovetskoe Stroitelstvo (Soviet Construction), periodical (formerly) of the USSR Central Executive Committee.

Sovetskaya Yustitsiya (Soviet Justice), periodical, organ of the RSFSR Ministry of Justice and the RSFSR Supreme Court.

Soviet Monitor, issued by *Tass*, London.

Soviet War News, organ of the Soviet Embassy, London.

Spasov, G., *Freedom of Religion in the USSR*, published by *Soviet News*, organ of the Soviet Embassy, London, 1951.

Stalin, J. V., *Problems of Leninism*, Foreign Languages Publishing House, Moscow, 1953.

Stalin, J. V.,*Works*, Foreign Languages Publishing House, Moscow, 13 volumes published, 1952–1955.

Timasheff, N. S., *Religion in Soviet Russia*, Sheed and Ward, London, 1944.

Trud (Labour), newspaper, organ of the All-Union Central Council of Trade Unions.

Tubert, Général, *L'Ouzbekistan, république soviétique*, Editions du Pavillon, Paris, 1951.

Turkmenskaya Iskra (Turkmenian Spark), newspaper, organ of the Central and the Ashkhabad Regional and Town Committees of the Communist Party of Turkmenia and of the Presidium of the Supreme Soviet of the Turkmenian SSR.

Uchitelskaya Gazeta (Teachers' Gazette newspaper, organ of the Ministry of Education CCCP and the Central Committee of the Trade Union of Education Workers.

Ugolovny Kodeks RSFSR (Criminal Codex of the RSFSR), State Publishing House of Juridical Literature, Moscow, 1953.

Ukrainian Bulletin, organ of the Ukrainian Congress Committee of America, New York.

USSR Information Bulletin, organ of the Soviet Embassy, Washington.

USSR Laws:
1924–1938: *Sobranie Zakonov i Rasporyazheniy Raboche-Krestyasnkogo Pravitelstva Soyuza Sovetskikh Sotsialisti-cheskikh Respublik* (Collection of Laws and Orders of the Worker-Peasant Government of the Union of Soviet Socialist Republics), Administration of Affairs of the Council of People's Commissars of the USSR, Moscow.

1938– ? : *Sobranie Postanovleniy i Rasporyazheniy Pravitelstva Soyuza Sovetskikh Sotsialisticheskikh Respublik* (Collection of Decrees and Orders of the Government of the Union of Soviet Socialist Republics), Administration of Affairs of the Council of People's Commissars (Council of Ministers from April, 1946) of the USSR, Moscow.

Vaitiekunas, Vytautas, *Genocide Against the Roman Catholic Church in Lithuania*, in *Baltic Review*, No. 2/3, June, 1954.

Vedomosti Verkhovnogo Soveta SSSR (The Gazette of the USSR Supreme Soviet), organ of the USSR Supreme Soviet.

Vedomosti Verkhovnogo Soveta RSFSR (The Gazette of the RSFSR Supreme Soviet), organ of the RSFSR Supreme Soviet.

Vestnik Russkogo Zapadno-Evropeiskogo Patriarshego Eksarkhata (Herald of the Russian Western European Patriarchal Exarchate), periodical, published in Paris.

Voprosy Filosofii (Questions of Philosophy), periodical, organ of the Institute of Philosophy of the USSR Academy of Sciences.

Voprosy Ideologicheskoi Raboty, Sbornik Vazhneishikh Resheniy KPSS (1954–1961) (Questions of Ideological Work, a Collection of the CPSU's Most Important Decisions (1954–1961)), State Publishing House of Political Literature, Moscow, 1961.

Voprosy Istorii Religii i Ateisma (Questions of the History of Religion and Atheism), No. 5, Publishing House of the USSR Academy of Sciences, Moscow, 1958.